The Socioeconomic Well-Being of California's Immigrant Youth

. . .

Laura E. Hill

2004

Public Policy Institute *of* California
1994–2004

Library of Congress Cataloging-in-Publication Data

Hill, Laura E., 1970-
  The socioeconomic well-being of California's immigrant youth /
Laura E. Hill.
    p. cm.
  Includes bibliographical references.
  ISBN: 1-58213-082-5
  1. Youth—California—Social conditions. 2. Youth—
California—Economic conditions. 3. Children of immigrants—
California. 4. Hispanic American youth—California. 5. Asian
American youth—California. 6. Youth with social disabilities—
California. I. Public Policy Institute of California. II. Title.

  HQ796.H488 2004
  305.235'09794—dc22   2004013033

Foreword

The public debate over U.S. immigration policy is often couched in simplistic terms. Immigrants are good for us because they keep us competitive in the global marketplace; or immigrants are bad for us because they suppress wages and consume too many public services. We rarely learn much about the immigrants themselves from these debates. In *The Socioeconomic Well-Being of California's Immigrant Youth*, however, Laura Hill offers a portrait of immigrant youth and shows why we should resist the lure of oversimplification.

Hill's report profiles the educational attainment, workforce participation, household arrangements, and parenting rates of California's immigrant youth. She finds that immigrants who arrive in the United States by age 10 tend to have outcomes similar to those for native-born youth of the same race and ethnicity. In contrast, the outcomes of later-arriving youth differ significantly from those of both their early-arriving counterparts and the native born; moreover, Hill notes, the outcomes for late-arriving Latinos are particularly worrisome. Geography also plays a key role. Central Coast immigrant youth, for example, frequently have worse outcomes than do their counterparts in Los Angeles and the San Joaquin Valley.

The public debate rarely focuses on age of arrival or regional geography, but for policymakers, these distinctions may be especially important. Hill concludes that in many cases, early-arriving immigrant youth can benefit from programs set up for their native-born peers. Both groups, for example, can be reached through public schools. Later-arriving youth are much more difficult to serve, however. Most are Latino, and many do not attend U.S. schools. Hill notes that reaching these late-arriving youth—through their children's schools, for example—and teaching them English language skills should be critical policy priorities.

Hill's work is a clear and useful description of the world of California's immigrant youth. It is also a mosaic of colors, textures, and patterns rather than an old-fashioned black and white photo. For these reasons, its findings can help ensure a balanced and accurate discussion of immigration policy.

David W. Lyon
President and CEO
Public Policy Institute of California

Summary

Californians direct substantial resources to youth between the ages of 13 and 24. Spending on schools, higher education, health insurance, after-school programs, and school-to-work programs accounts for a sizable portion of the state budget. The rationale for this spending is that opportunities and well-being during this transition to adulthood are likely to have far-reaching consequences. Not all California youth are making this transition in the same way, however. In particular, immigrant youth and the children of immigrants—who together make up half the state's population—are finishing high school, entering the labor market, beginning college, and starting families in different orders, at different paces, and with different levels of success than are many native-born youth.

How are California's immigrant youth faring as they make the transition to adulthood? This report's findings point to four important themes. First, immigrant youth who arrive by age 10 appear to have educational and labor market outcomes similar to those of native-born youth of the same race or ethnicity. Second, immigrant youth who arrive at older ages have outcomes very different from those who arrive before age 10. These outcomes vary significantly by race and ethnicity. On average, Hispanic immigrants arriving over age 10 fare poorly, and Asian immigrants fare well. Third, outcomes for third and higher generations vary quite dramatically by race and ethnicity. In other words, racial and ethnic differences persist even among the grandchildren and great grandchildren of immigrants. Finally, the experience of immigrant youth is not the same in all parts of the state. A large share of immigrant youth in the Central Coast region, for example, fares poorly on many measures such as poverty and spoken English ability. Indeed, their outcomes are often worse than those for youth in regions with equal shares (and larger numbers) of young immigrants, such as Los Angeles County and the San Joaquin Valley.

Early-Arriving Immigrant Youth

Immigrant youth who arrive in the United States before age 10 usually come with their parents and attend schools here. For these youth, patterns of school enrollment and work effort are similar to those of second-generation youth within each race and ethnic group. This is especially good news because more than half of all immigrant youth arrive before age 10. Hispanic youth currently ages 19 to 24 who arrived before age 10 have attended college in nearly equal proportions as their second-generation counterparts—33 versus 41 percent—whereas only 13 percent of late-arriving immigrants do so (see Figure S.1).

The same pattern holds for Asian immigrant youth: 78 percent of those who arrived before age 10 have attended some college by the time they are 19 to 24 years old, as have 80 percent of second-generation Asian youth. English language ability among early-arriving Hispanics is quite comparable to that of second-generation Hispanic youth (11% versus 4%) by the same age. Similarly, the percentage of youth who

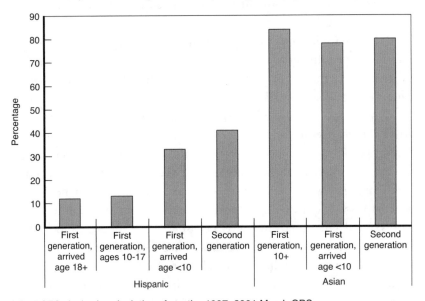

SOURCES: Author's calculations from the 1997–2001 March CPS.

Figure S.1—Percentage of California Hispanic and Asian Youth Ages 19 to 24 Who Have Attended At Least Some College, by Generation

have become parents is virtually identical among second-generation and early arriving Hispanic immigrant women; approximately one-third of each are living with their own children at ages 19 to 24.

Late-Arriving Immigrant Youth

Whereas early-arriving immigrant youth resemble their second-generation counterparts, late-arriving immigrant youth exhibit striking variations in outcomes. Over one-third of all Hispanic youth ages 19 to 24 are immigrants who arrived at age 10 or later; the comparable figure for all Asian and Pacific Islander youth is more than one-quarter.

In general, late-arriving Asian immigrant youth fare well. School enrollment rates are high, and at least 84 percent have attended some college. Late-arriving Hispanic youth do not fare nearly as well. Many appear to by-pass school altogether, instead focusing on the world of work. About 10 percent have attended some college, and many more have less than a ninth grade education. Nearly two-thirds do not speak English fluently, and 64 percent lack health insurance compared to 35 percent of Asians. Late-arriving Hispanic youth are also very likely to have started families. Nearly half of young women ages 19 to 24 are living with their own children, whereas parenting rates for Asian immigrant youth are negligible.

Third-Generation Youth

Outcomes for third-generation youth differ greatly across racial and ethnic boundaries. Third-generation Hispanic youth, for example, are still considerably less likely than white or Asian youth to have attended some college and are more likely to be working and not attending school. Twenty-three percent of Hispanic third-generation youth lack health insurance as opposed to 16 percent of their Asian and white counterparts. Parenting rates among Hispanics are dramatically higher as well—40 percent versus 20 percent among third-generation whites. These disparities suggest that gaps among yesterday's first-generation youth did not close by the third generation or that disparities grew over time in the United States.

Regional Differences

As expected, Los Angeles and the San Joaquin Valley showed large concentrations of immigrant youth and relatively poor youth outcomes. However, these are not the only regions with high proportions of poor immigrant youth. Indeed, the highest concentrations of immigrant youth are in the Central Coast, where most are between ages 19 and 24 and few are college students. Many migrated as young adults. The percentage of youth who arrived in the United States after age 18 is higher in the Central Coast than in Los Angeles County, the San Diego region, or the San Joaquin Valley.

On average, Central Coast youth appear to be as well educated as youth elsewhere in the state; approximately the same proportion has earned at least a high school degree. These averages mask substantial variation, however, as the Central Coast is home to both the least and most educated youth in the state. About 10 percent of youth between ages 19 and 24 have less than a high school education (a higher percentage than in the San Joaquin Valley), but nearly seven in ten have at least some college education (a higher percentage than in the Bay Area).

English proficiency among high school students is somewhat higher in the Central Coast than in other regions that typically receive large numbers of new immigrants. However, this fact does not mean that the school-aged population is doing well. Many young people of school age are not enrolled in the Central Coast. In fact, the Central Coast's immigrant youth ages 16 to 24 have the state's lowest enrollment rates among immigrant youth (Table S.1).

When the overall youth population is considered, the Central Coast ranks lowest in the state in English language ability; more than 20 percent self-report that they are not fluent in English.

The overall poverty level in the Central Coast, 17 percent, is similar to that for Los Angeles County but far below that for the San Joaquin Valley. However, youth poverty rates are considerably higher—about 25 percent. This is equal to the rate for the San Joaquin Valley and higher than that for Los Angeles. Despite their similar levels of poverty, youth

Table S.1

Percentage of First-Generation California Youth Ages 16 to 24 Not Enrolled in School, by Region

	Percentage
Bay Area	42
Central Coast	78
Inland Empire	52
Los Angeles County	56
Orange County	59
Sacramento Metro	36
San Diego	57
San Joaquin Valley	58

SOURCES: Author's Calculations from the 1997–2000 October CPS.

in the San Joaquin Valley are much more likely than their Central Coast counterparts to receive public assistance. The Central Coast's affluent, older population balances out the younger, struggling population to create a demographic profile in line with that for the rest of the state. The reality is, however, that the Central Coast is home to a disproportionate share of Hispanic immigrant youth who are poor, not well educated, not fluent in English, and unlikely to receive welfare despite their high needs.

Policies that address the needs of second- and third-generation youth are also likely to help early-arriving immigrant youth and late-arriving youth who attend school. The majority of programs, however, cannot assist first-generation youth who are not in school, because so many programs are school-based. Instead, these out-of-school youth must be reached through their employers or through the schools that their children attend.

Contents

Figures

Tables

Acknowledgments

I would like to thank the many people who provided thoughtful reviews of this report: Deborah Reed, Patricia de Cos, Arturo Gonzalez, Christopher Jepsen, and Hans Johnson. The invaluable research assistance of Joseph Hayes also helped make this report possible. Anne Danenberg's able assistance is also greatly appreciated. The report also benefited from comments from my other colleagues at PPIC and members of PPIC's Advisory Council. Finally, Peter Richardson's editorial improvements are much appreciated. Although this report reflects the contributions of many people, I am solely responsible for its content.

1. Introduction

California has a large and disadvantaged population of youth ages 13 to 24. That population also has a large number of immigrants and the children of immigrants who are generally financially worse off than their native-born counterparts. For example, 31 percent of immigrant youth live below the poverty line, whereas 17 percent of native-born youth are poor. Among Hispanic youth, the foreign-born are more likely than the native-born to drop out of high school (Driscoll, 1999). Other indicators, such as high levels of teen parenthood and low college graduation rates, also suggest problems in preparing California's immigrant youth for increased economic stability.

The ages 13 to 24 are crucial years for making a successful entry into adult life. Californians already invest a great deal of resources in this age group through schools, health care programs, pregnancy and drug prevention, and a host of other programs. However, it is not clear that these expenditures reach the group most in need. The two institutions we rely on most to smooth the transition from childhood to adulthood—the educational system and families—may not function well for immigrant youth. Some older immigrant youth may come to the United States without their families and may never enroll in California's schools. Vernez and Mizell (2001) estimate that there are 100,000 Hispanic immigrants ages 15 to 17 not enrolled in school in the United States at any point in time. These youth are particularly likely to enter the workforce with little education and poor English skills, and they are also among the most likely to have children at young ages. For these and other reasons, it is critical not only to understand how they are faring but also to know where they live and how their educational outcomes and job prospects might be improved.

Research at the national level does not often distinguish among outcomes for immigrants by state and certainly does not break down the analysis to the regional level. We therefore have much to learn about how immigrant youth are faring not only in Los Angeles County and the Bay Area but also in less common immigrant-receiving areas and over successive generations. More important, much of the existing research treats immigrants and their children as a monolithic group, making no distinction between racial and ethnic subgroups. The purpose of this descriptive report is to highlight well-being among immigrant youth in California. Our data allow us to examine differences among white, Asian, and Hispanic immigrants; to evaluate outcomes by age of arrival in this country; and to distinguish between the native-born children of immigrants (second-generation) and the native-born children of the native-born (third-generation plus). The report also presents results for the state's major regions. A limitation of this report is that it covers just one period, 1997–2001. As a result, outcomes measured among immigrant youth may be unique to this cohort or a by-product of the economic and social conditions faced by them during this period.

In the remainder of the report, the demographic characteristics, household and family characteristics, and educational attainment and activities of Hispanic, non-Hispanic Asian and Pacific Islander, and non-Hispanic white immigrant and native-born youth are described and compared. Sample size is insufficient to include non-Hispanic blacks (blacks) and non-Hispanic American Indians (American Indians) in this report. A very small share of each is foreign-born. Readers should note that Asians are a very diverse group and can have widely divergent outcomes depending on country of origin. For example, Southeast Asian foreign-born youth have much higher poverty rates than foreign-born youth from the rest of Asia (37% versus 19%). Sample size is insufficient to separate the Asian subgroups (such as East and Southeast Asians) in this report. However, other PPIC reports, such as *A Portrait of Race and Ethnicity in California* (Reyes, 2001) include detail for both Asian subgroups and for Native Americans. The multiracial population is not described here because the main data source used for this report (Current Population Survey—CPS) permits respondents to choose only one race.

Often when researchers compare second and third generations to the first generation using cross-sectional data, they use such terms as "progress," "stagnation," or even "negative assimilation." To appropriately call such differences progress, we need longitudinal data to follow immigrants as they age, compare children to their own parents, or use repeated cross-sections of data. This report focuses on just five years of data (1997–2001) and one age group (13 to 24); thus, differences observed across generations cannot be reliably described as either progress or negative assimilation. In cross-sectional data, first-generation immigrants may be from very different sending countries than the second-generation youth to whom they are compared. Thus, any observed variations in outcomes among the generations might be attributable entirely to differences in the national origin composition of each generation. Among Hispanics, this is less problematic because almost all California Hispanics descend from those born in Mexico or Central America, but by the third generation, self-identification by race and ethnicity becomes more amorphous. A sense of identification with a cultural heritage may decline over the generations, and people have more racial and ethnic groups to affiliate with because of intermarriage. Research has also suggested that those who choose to identify as Hispanics are generally of lower socioeconomic status than those of the same ancestral background but who choose an alternative racial or ethnic identification (Portes and MacLeod, 1996, Eschbach and Gomez, 1998). Thus, although it is tempting to call differences between generations progress or negative assimilation, we avoid this terminology. Instead, we focus on differences among first-generation youth (based on age at arrival and race and ethnicity) and among third-generation youth (based on race and ethnicity rather than on comparisons between first-generation youth and their third-generation counterparts.

Unless otherwise noted, the tables and figures in this report are for California youth only. Group differences discussed in the text are statistically significant at the 5 percent level unless otherwise noted. Figures and tables generally do not include sample sizes—see Tables A.1 and A.3 in the appendix for sample sizes of breakdowns used frequently in this report.

The rest of the report is organized as follows. Chapter 2 describes California's immigrant youth population, contrasting the demographic characteristics of foreign-born youth, such as racial and ethnic groups, age, and language, to those of the native-born. Chapter 3 explores household and family arrangements and resource levels for these new Californians. Chapter 4 addresses the activities of these youth (school, work, parenting), as well as their educational attainment, drawing important distinctions by immigrant generation, sex, and race. Chapter 5 focuses on regional differences in some of these outcomes. Presenting results in this manner helps policymakers and researchers understand which regions, institutions, and generations (analyzed by race and ethnicity) may need to be targeted to improve outcomes for California's immigrant youth. Chapter 6 concludes the report with suggestions for such targeting.

2. Who Are California's Youth?

California's youth are a large and growing segment of the population. In 2000, youth ages 13 to 24 numbered 5.6 million, or approximately 17 percent of the state's population. By 2010, that share is expected to grow to 18 percent (State of California 1998). Nearly one-quarter of California's youth are foreign-born compared with only 8 percent of youth in the rest of the United States (Figure 2.1). Another one-quarter of California's youth are native-born but have at least one foreign-born parent; that figure is only 8 percent for youth in other states. Youth are four times as likely as children to be foreign-born in California (24% versus 6%). California adults are more likely than California's youth to be foreign-born but less likely to be second generation. The high percentage of first-generation youth both necessitates and allows in-depth analysis of the outcomes for youth by generation in California.

Generation

Research on immigrant adaptation has found that immigrants who arrive in the United States while still young are much more likely than those who immigrated after age 10 to have outcomes such as educational attainment and fertility levels similar to those of natives (Portes and Rumbaut 2001; Hill and Johnson, 2002). Ramakrishnan (2004) finds that native-born youth with only one foreign-born parent have better socioeconomic outcomes than do native-born youth with two foreign-born parents. Thus, this report distinguishes among multiple generations wherever possible.

As Figure 2.1 shows, a slight majority of the state's youth is third or higher generation, meaning that over half were born in the United States to native-born parents. The remaining half are nearly equally divided

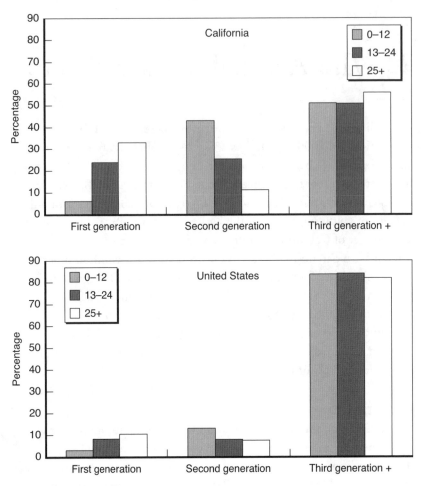

SOURCES: Author's calculations from the 1997–2001 March CPS.

Figure 2.1—Percentage in Each Generation, by Age: California and the Rest of the United States

between first generation (foreign-born) and second generation. When the first generation is refined to consider age at arrival (Table 2.1), 12 percent of California's youth arrived before age 10, 8 percent between

Table 2.1

California Youth Ages 13 to 24, by Generation

Generation	Percentage
First, arrived age 18+	3
First, arrived ages 10–17	8
First, arrived age <10	12
Second, two foreign-born parents	18
Second, one foreign-born parent	7
Third+	51
	100

SOURCES: Author's calculations from the 1997–2001 March CPS.

ages 10 and 17, and the remaining 3 percent after age 18.[1] For the most part, youth who arrive in the United States before age 10 have received at least some of their education in the United States. Not all youth who arrive between the ages of 10 and 17 enroll in U.S. schools, and those who arrive at age 18 or older do not enroll in U.S. high schools. These distinctions may be important in our efforts to understand whether the resources we direct toward youth reach California's immigrant youth. In the second generation, youth are much more likely to have two foreign-born parents (2.0 generation) than only one (2.5 generation), probably because of the high rates of intermarriage among immigrants.

Race and Ethnicity

Hispanic youth are the most common group among California's youth—nearly 2.5 million Hispanic youth were counted in the 2000 Census, accounting for 41 percent of the youth population (Hispanics are approximately one-third of the total California population). Whites are almost a majority of the total California population (47% in 2000) but account for just 37 percent of the youth population.

---

[1]There is some degree of uncertainty about the exact age at arrival in the CPS data. Responses are coded into two, three, or five-year bands of arrival. Because this report focuses on a younger population, uncertainty about age at arrival is lower—most immigrant youth arrived relatively recently (1980 or later), and the CPS codes their year of arrival into two or three-year bands, rather than five-year bands.

Fewer than 10 percent of black youth are foreign-born (Figure 2.2). An even smaller share of white youth are foreign-born (6%). In contrast, most Hispanic and Asian youth are either immigrants or the children of immigrants. Taken as a group, immigrant youth are primarily Hispanic (62%) and Asian (25%). Similarly, most third-generation youth are white.

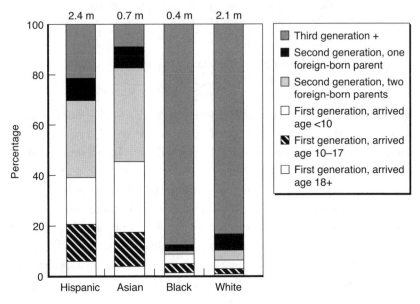

SOURCES: Author's calculations from the 1997–2001 March CPS and Census 2000.

Figure 2.2—Percentage of California Youth Ages 13 to 24 in Each Generation, by Race and Ethnic Group

Age and Age at Arrival

Immigrants are most likely to move to the United States in their teens and twenties (Hill and Hayes, 2003). Thus, the share of youth who are foreign-born increases with age. This is especially true among California's Hispanics and Asians. At ages 13 to 15, approximately one-quarter of Hispanics are foreign-born, but by ages 19 to 24, that figure rises to one-half (Figure 2.3). The increase is similar for Asians: the

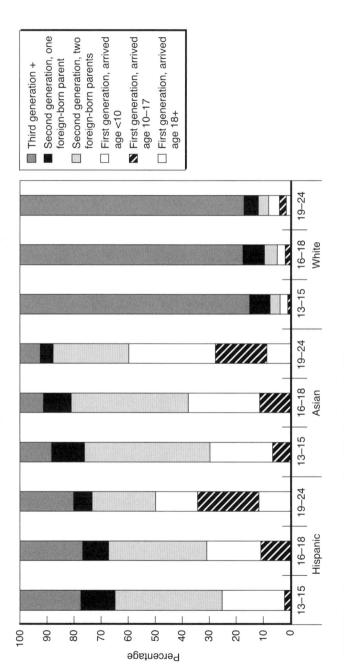

Legend:
- Third generation +
- Second generation, one foreign-born parent
- Second generation, two foreign-born parents
- First generation, arrived age <10
- First generation, arrived age 10–17
- First generation, arrived age 18+

SOURCES: Author's calculations from the 1997–2001 March CPS.

Figure 2.3—Percentage of California Youth Ages 13 to 24 in Each Generation, by Age, Race, and Ethnic Group

foreign-born share increases to 60 percent by ages 19 to 24 from less than 30 percent at ages 13 to 15. More than one-third of Hispanic youth ages 19 to 24 arrived in the United States after age 10 and 12 percent after age 17. The number for Asian youth is nearly 30 percent and 9 percent after age 17. These youth are the least likely to have attended U.S. high schools.

Because the teens and early twenties are common ages for migration, older immigrant youth in California have actually been in the United States for shorter periods than have younger immigrant youth. Seventeen percent of California immigrant youth ages 19 to 24 arrived in California within the last two years, as opposed to 10 percent of California youth ages 13 to 15 (Table 2.2). Many immigrant youth who migrated after age 16 may never have been enrolled in U.S. schools, although some likely migrated to attend college. Nearly one-third of those ages 19 to 24 arrived in the United States after the age of 16. Overall, slightly more than half of our sample of youth is male: 51 percent. When we look just at immigrant youth, we find that 53 percent are male.

Table 2.2

**Length of Time in the United States of California
Foreign-Born Youth, by Age**

	Age Distribution (%)		
Years in the United States	13–15	16–18	19–24
0 to 2	10	14	17
3 to 5	14	10	11
6+	76	76	71
	100	100	100

SOURCES: Author's calculations from the 1997–2001 March CPS.

Language

Although one in four youth is foreign-born, the vast majority of youth are fluent English speakers (91%). Among those who are not fluent in English, nearly all are Spanish speakers (95%), although this is likely because the CPS is administered only in English and Spanish.

Respondents who are speakers of Asian and other languages who are not fluent in English are more likely to be excluded from the data collection. However, the effect appears to be small. An analysis of 2000 Census data found that 92 percent of youth are fluent English speakers. Among the non-fluent, only 90 percent speak Spanish (as opposed to 95% in the CPS). Of the 10 percent who speak a language other than Spanish, 1.5 percent speak Chinese, 1.3 percent speak Vietnamese, and less than 1 percent each speak Korean, Japanese, and Filipino. Despite these differences in language distribution between the CPS and the Census, the California CPS sample of Asian immigrants and the California Asian immigrants enumerated in the 2000 Census are virtually identical in their distribution by place of birth.

Almost all youth who do not speak English fluently are in the first generation. Somewhat more than 10 percent of foreign-born youth ages 13 to 18 are not fluent in English, according to the CPS. However, at older ages (19 to 24), more than 40 percent of foreign-born youth are not fluent (Figure 2.4). This group is made up of newer arrivals to the

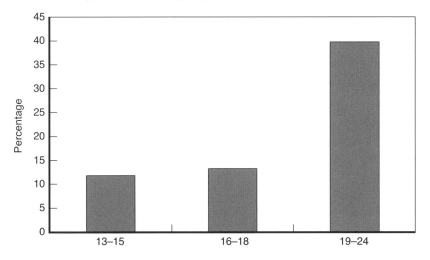

SOURCE: Author's calculations from the 1999 October CPS.

Figure 2.4—Percentage of First-Generation California Youth Not Fluent in English, by Age

United States, many of whom never entered schools here after migrating. They will no doubt gain experience with English over time and as they are exposed to the language in the workplace and communities. Doing so is important to economic advancement—English language skills bear a strong association with labor market progress for the foreign-born (Carnevale, Fry, and Lowell, 2001; Gonzalez, 2000).

Because the CPS is administered in Spanish, language detail should be more reliable among Hispanics. Among Hispanic youth, more than 80 percent of those who arrive at ages 18 or older are not fluent in English, and more than half are reported to be in households where every adult member speaks only Spanish (Table 2.3). Among those who arrived between ages 10 and 17, slightly more than half are not fluent in English. However, among those who arrived before age 10, only 11 percent of Hispanic youth are not fluent, but more than one-third still speak only Spanish at home. From Table 2.3, it does not appear that speaking only Spanish in the home is a barrier to learning English. Indeed, Portes and Rumbaut (2001) find that speaking a foreign language at home is associated with strong school performance for some groups of children of immigrants. By the second generation, virtually all Hispanic youth are fluent in English, but approximately one-fifth are reported to reside in households where all adult members speak only Spanish. However, in comparison to Hispanic immigrant youth at the

Table 2.3

Language Detail for California Hispanic Youth Ages 13 to 24

Generation	% Not Fluent in English (a)	% in Spanish- Speaking Households (b)
First, arrived age 18+	83	55
First, arrived ages 10–17	53	46
First, arrived age <10	11	35
Second, two foreign-born parents	4	19
Second, one foreign-born parent	4	3
Third+	3	1

SOURCE: Author's calculations from the 1999 October CPS (a) and the 1997–2001 October CPS (b).

national level, California's Hispanic immigrants are less likely to be fluent in English. Nationally, over half of Hispanic immigrant youth arriving after age 10 are already English fluent (not shown).

California's immigrant youth are a large fraction of the state's population, and 87 percent are Hispanic or Asian. As English fluency levels demonstrate, outcomes for these two groups of immigrant youth can be quite different. Older immigrant youth make up a greater share of the more recent arrivals to the United States, and they appear to have the greatest difficulty with the English language. This is especially true for Hispanic immigrant youth arriving after the age of 17. Youth who arrive at younger ages (under age 10) appear to have English language skills that are closer to those of second-generation youth than to those of immigrants arriving after age 10 or later.

3. What Are the Living Arrangements and Resources of Immigrant Youth?

This chapter asks the following questions: at what ages do immigrant youth start their own families and households? Are recent arrivals to the United States more likely than other immigrants and other youth to live on their own or with roommates? How likely are immigrant youth to be living with both of their parents? How much lower are the resource levels of immigrant youth relative to their native-born counterparts? How do resources vary by race and ethnicity? The answers to these questions might highlight the ways policymakers could address resource differentials.

Resource levels are explored by examining poverty status, welfare use, parental work effort, and parental education levels (for those still residing with their parents). Resource levels are likely to be associated with family and household arrangements. For example, resources levels are generally higher in two-parent families (Reed and Swearingen, 2001), as is school success among children (Vandivere, Moore, and Brown, 2000).

Another crucial consideration for immigrant youth is the citizenship mix of their families. Eligibility for many federal and state programs is based on legal status, and benefit levels for families therefore depend both on the resource needs and on the number of legal, eligible members. Citizenship is examined as a proxy for legal status. Finally, health status, health insurance, and mortality are examined, as well as telephone and computer access.

Household Arrangements

Almost all youth ages 13 to 15 (95%) live with one parent or more and are not yet heading families (not shown). At ages 16 to 18 also, the vast majority of youth still live with at least one parent. This is true for over 90 percent of second- and third-generation youth and more than 75 percent of first generation youth (Figure 3.1). First-generation youth are more likely than the native-born to live with other relatives, alone or with roommates, and to have started their own families, either as a head of household or as a head of a family in a larger household (4% and 3%, respectively, or 7% total),[1] suggesting that many are in the United States without their parents. Only 4 percent of the second generation and 2 percent of the third generation have started their own families. Hispanic immigrant youth appear to be more likely than Asian or white immigrant youth to be family heads. However, these results were not statistically significant and are not shown here.

At older ages (19 to 24), household arrangements can be investigated in greater detail (Figure 3.2). Some patterns span all racial and ethnic groups. Second-generation youth are more likely than first-generation youth to live with their parents. Between the second and third generation, the pattern reverses. First-generation youth may live without their parents at a higher rate than in other generations because many may have come without parents (to work or study in the United States) or because many immigrants who arrived at age 10 are parents. Each explanation will be explored in the next chapter. The lower levels of co-residence with parents in third generation versus the second may be a result of increasing college attendance and financial independence; third-generation youth are the most likely to live on their own or with

---

[1]Youth who head primary families are "heads of household" and those who head subfamilies are "heads of family." Youth who are married to family or household heads are also included in these categories. Youth who are not family heads and live with their parents are in the "live with own parent(s)" group; those who are not family heads and who live with relatives (not their parents) are in the "live with other relative(s)" group. Youth who do not head families and who live with parents or relatives are "dependent youth." The final category is youth who "live alone or with roommates." It is possible that youth in the "head of family" category actually still live with their parents or relatives. Those who live in group quarters (n = 23) are excluded from this analysis.

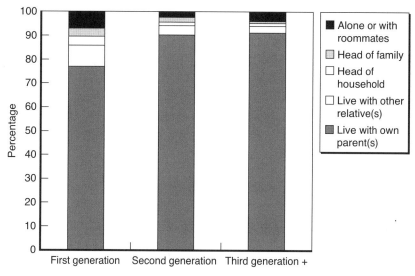

SOURCES: Author's calculations from the 1997–2001 March CPS.

Figure 3.1—Living Arrangements of California Youth Ages 16 to 18, by Generation: Hispanic, Asian, and White Combined

roommates (with the exception of first-generation Hispanics arriving after the age of 17).

Within racial and ethnic groups, interesting patterns emerge. Hispanic youth are the most likely to have become family heads, regardless of generation. Among first-generation Hispanic youth who arrived after age 10, starting a family, either as a household head or as a family head, is quite common. However, first-generation Hispanics who arrived after age 17 are slightly less likely than those foreign-born Hispanics who arrived between the ages of 10 and 17 to have started their own families (41% versus 44%). These youth may have yet to acquire the resources necessary to begin a family. In total, only about one-quarter of Hispanic first-generation youth live with their parents. Hispanic first-generation youth are the least likely of first-generation youth to live alone or with roommates—this group of immigrants is highly likely to be connected to an extended family or to have begun their own families. Most interesting is the similarity between Hispanic first generation youth

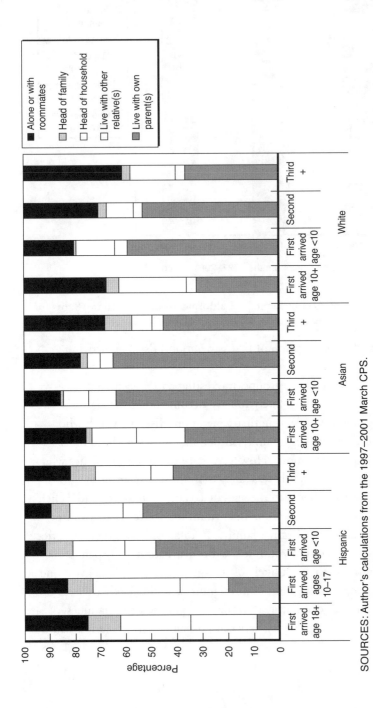

SOURCES: Author's calculations from the 1997–2001 March CPS.

Figure 3.2—Living Arrangements of California Youth Ages 19 to 24, by Generation and Race/Ethnicity

arriving under age 10 and their native-born counterparts: Nearly an equal percentage are living with their own parents.

Asian youth are the least likely of all youth to have become family or household heads and are much more likely than Hispanic youth to live with their own parents. Like Hispanic immigrant youth, Asian immigrant youth who arrive under age 10 live with their own parents in similar proportion to second-generation Asian youth.

Although the living arrangements of first-generation youth arriving by age 10 are similar to the arrangements of second-generation youth within the same race or ethnic group, differences persist across the groups in the third generation. White third-generation youth live alone (or with roommates) or with their parents. Few have started their own families or households. Hispanic youth are more likely than whites or Asians to have started families or households (32% for Hispanics, 19% and 21% for Asians and whites, respectively).

Family Structure for Dependent Youth

Previous research has demonstrated the financial and emotional value to children of living with two parents. Children raised in two-parent families do better in school and have fewer behavioral problems (Vandivere, Moore, and Brown, 2000; McLanahan, 1997). Children living in two-parent families also have lower poverty rates (Reed and Swearingen, 2001). Children of immigrants (first- and second-generation youth) may be less likely to live with both parents because migration itself often separates spouses (sons may migrate with their fathers, for instance) and may lead to stresses in marriage and divorce (Hill, 2004). On the other hand, because immigrants typically come from countries where divorce and nonmarital childbearing are uncommon, children of immigrants could live with both parents more commonly than third-generation youth.

Asian youth are the most likely of the racial and ethnic groups to live with both parents (Figure 3.3). When we consider racial and ethnic groups and generation simultaneously, we find that Hispanic children of immigrants (first and second generation) are more likely than third-generation Hispanics to live with both parents. For Hispanics, it is possible that any family disruption resulting from migration in the first

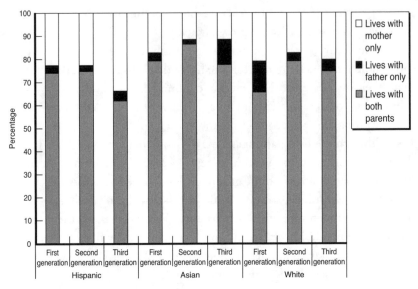

SOURCES: Author's calculations from the 1997–2001 March CPS.

Figure 3.3—Living Arrangements of California Youth Ages 13 to 24, Co-Resident with at Least One Parent

or second generation is smaller in magnitude than greater disruptions among subsequent generations, such as family dissolution and nonmarital childbearing. The share of youth who live only with one parent is lower in the first than in the second generation for Asians and whites, suggesting that these first-generation youth experience family disruption because of migration (although this difference between the first and second generation is not statistically significant for whites).

Living with only one's father is relatively uncommon across all groups. Hispanic youth are more likely than whites and Asians to live with only their mothers in each generation. In the third generation, they are also more likely than first- or second-generation Hispanics to live only with their mothers. Brandon (2002) found this same pattern for third generation Mexican children relative to first and second generation, even when he controlled for socioeconomic status. He also found that third-generation Mexican youth are less likely than third-generation white children to live in two-parent families, as is shown in Figure 3.3.

The relationship between family structure and poverty is examined below.

Poverty

A commonly used measure of economic well-being, poverty, is measured at the family level. Since the 1950s, a family is considered to be poor if its income is less than three times the food budget required to feed a family nutritiously. Regional variations in prices, such as housing, are not considered. The only variations the measure incorporates are age and family size. Many argue that this poverty measure vastly understates the hardship experienced by low-income families (Citro and Michaels, 1995). Food costs have fallen, but housing and new costs, such as telecommunications and child care, have risen. This report uses the standard poverty measure because it is important to compare these results with those from other national-and state-level studies. However, changes in the definition of poverty that consider the higher costs of housing in the state increase the chances that a Californian is classified as living in poverty (Reed and Swearingen, 2001).

Within the first generation, age at arrival is associated with better outcomes among Asians and whites and less so among Hispanics. Asians and whites who arrived by age 10 have poverty rates more like those of the second generation than those of the foreign-born who arrived later than age 10. This is not the case for Hispanics. We might expect third-generation youth to have substantially lower levels of poverty than second and first generation youth because they and their parents are U.S.-educated. However, white and Asian youth actually have higher poverty rates in the third generation than in the second-generation (Figure 3.4).[2] Rather than demonstrating a lack of "progress" among the native-born, these results seem to illustrate the difficulty in comparing generations in a cross-section (i.e., without comparing third-

---

[2]These estimates consider the age distribution of youth within each generation because younger youth are more likely to live with their parents and are therefore less likely to be poor. First-generation youth are older than third-generation youth, so controlling for age helps isolate by generation the differences in poverty that are due to factors other than age. To do so, regression models predict poverty by generation, race, ethnicity, and age. Estimates where college students were excluded did not vary.

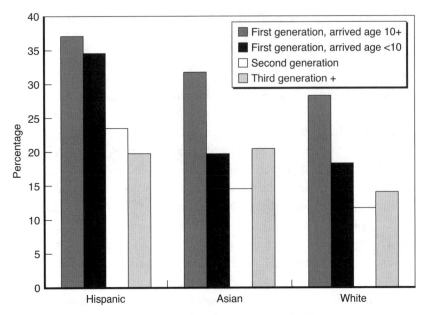

SOURCES: Author's calculations from the 1997–2001 March CPS.
NOTE: Results are age-standardized.

Figure 3.4—Poverty Among California Youth Ages 13 to 24, by Generation and Race/Ethnicity

generation youth to second-generation from an earlier period, we cannot assess whether they are faring better or worse than their predecessors).

Previous research demonstrates that household and family arrangements are related to resource levels in the family. Recall from Figures 3.1 and 3.2 that higher proportions of white and Asian youth live alone or with roommates (especially by the third generation), which may explain the higher rates of poverty in the third generation than in the second. An examination of poverty status by household structure, race, and generation revealed that the percentage of poor youth who still reside with parents or other relatives is lower for each successive generation for all races (not shown). Higher poverty levels for white and Asian third-generation youth than among second-generation youth may be related to earlier efforts to assert financial and familial independence—efforts that may be more likely to increase with time in the United States.

Typically, poverty levels are lower in two-parent families than in single-parent families. When only youth living in two-parent families are examined, poverty is lower for each successive generation, for each race and ethnic group (Figure 3.5). Immigrant youth in two-parent families are much more likely than native-born youth in two-parent families to live in poverty, even when the age structure of each generation is considered (see footnote 2). This is true for Hispanic, white, and Asian youth alike, although the results for Asian youth are not statistically significant. The poverty gap is smaller between children of immigrants and natives who live with single parents. Reardon-Anderson, Capps, and Fix (2002) also find that being in a two-parent family does not appear to provide the same income advantage for children of immigrants as it does for the children of natives. Children of immigrants are still twice as likely as children of natives to live below 200 percent of the poverty line.

Welfare Use

Because of their lower rates of eligibility and older age structure, immigrant youth will receive welfare at lower rates than expected from their poverty status alone. Even controlling for current age (as in footnote 2), foreign-born youth who arrive after age 10 have the highest poverty rates but some of the lowest rates of public assistance receipt (Figure 3.6). Among Hispanics, youth are more likely to be in families that receive welfare if they are first-generation immigrants who arrived before age 10 or if they are second or third generation, regardless of lower rates of poverty. Despite lower levels of need, Hispanic youth are more likely to benefit from public assistance in later generations. This pattern is likely due to increases in eligibility based on legal status rather than to increasing resource needs. Asian and white youth are the most likely to receive welfare if they are immigrants arriving before age 10 and substantially less likely in all other generations.

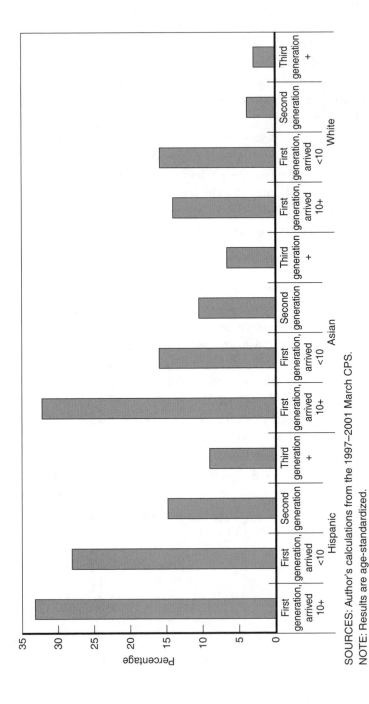

SOURCES: Author's calculations from the 1997–2001 March CPS.

NOTE: Results are age-standardized.

Figure 3.5—Poverty Among California Youth Ages 13 to 24 in Two-Parent Families, by Generation and Race/Ethnicity

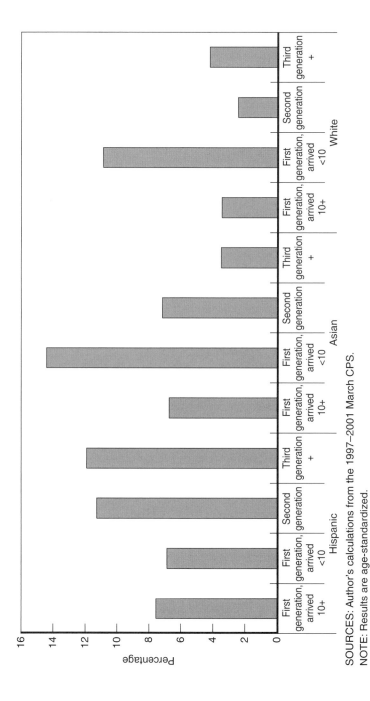

SOURCES: Author's calculations from the 1997–2001 March CPS.
NOTE: Results are age-standardized.

Figure 3.6—Welfare Receipt Among Families of California Youth Ages 13 to 24, by Generation and Race/Ethnicity

Citizenship Mix of Youth Households

Citizenship status, although not synonymous with legal status, is correlated with it. Legal immigrants and their families enjoy greater rights and privileges in their ability to work and to qualify for certain benefits, such as Temporary Assistance for Needy Families (TANF). Legalization is associated with upward mobility in job status, although the effect of legal status is greater for women than men (Powers, Seltzer, and Shi, 1998). Although citizenship is not required for TANF eligibility, not all citizen immigrants are eligible.[3] Data on eligibility status are not available in the CPS. Therefore, we use citizenship and mixed citizenship status as a sort of proxy for eligibility, as in Fix and Zimmermann (2001).

All third-generation family members are likely to be citizens. However, some second-generation youth will have non-citizen parents. In the case of youth under the age of 18 still living with parents or relatives, citizenship status is considered in conjunction with that of parents or guardians. The children of youth who have started their own families are included in the definition of family citizenship. For youth age 18 and older who have not started their own families, only their own citizenship status is considered, even if they still live with parents or relatives. A family is defined as a "citizen" family if all of its members are citizens, a "noncitizen" family if all members are noncitizens, and "mixed" if at least one child is a citizen and at least one parent is a noncitizen, following the example of Fix and Zimmermann (2001).[4]

Family citizenship status varies greatly by race and generation. Many fewer Hispanic children than white and Asian children are in citizen families (Figure 3.7). In the first generation, less than 10 percent of Hispanic youth are in citizen families, compared to over one-third of both white and Asian youth. Close to one-third of Hispanic first-generation youth are in mixed-status families (a much higher proportion

---

[3]Lawful permanent residents, refugees, and other protected classes are eligible. See http://www.nilc.org/ciwc/ciwc_ce/CalWorks.htm for a complete discussion.

[4]Families in which all children are noncitizens and at least one parent is a citizen do not exist in this sample. Furthermore, because the benefits for TANF and other assistance programs for families hinge on the eligibility of the children (e.g., citizenship), a family would not be eligible for assistance if its children were noncitizens.

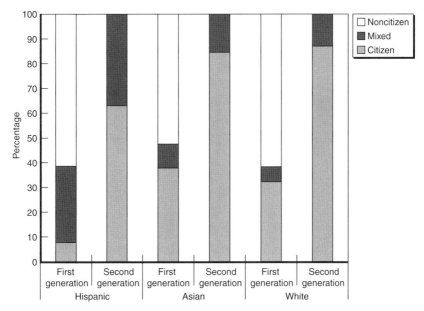

SOURCES: Author's calculations from the 1997–2001 March CPS.

Figure 3.7—Family Citizenship Status of California Youth Ages 13 to 24, by Generation and Race/Ethnicity

than for Asian and white youth), which brings the total share of Hispanic youth with at least one citizen member to close to the share for whites and Asian youth. However, the number of eligible family members, not just the presence of one eligible member, determines public assistance benefit levels. In the second generation, Hispanic youth are more likely than Asian and white youth to be members of mixed-status citizen families. In the rest of the United States, Hispanic first generation youth are considerably more likely to be in citizen families than they are in California (22% versus 8%), as are white first-generation youth (45% versus 32%).

Citizenship status is also related to poverty among immigrant families. The poor are disproportionately made up of mixed citizen and noncitizen families, whereas youth in families made up entirely of citizens are much more likely to be in families receiving welfare (Figure 3.8).

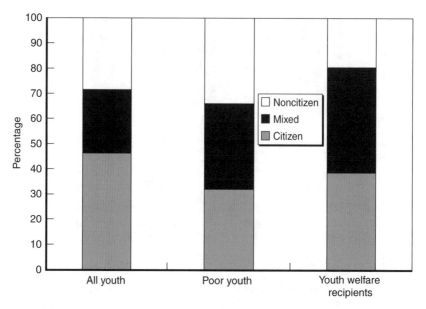

SOURCES: Author's calculations from the 1997–2001 March CPS.

Figure 3.8—Family Citizenship Mix of First- and Second-Generation
California Youth Ages 13 to 24: All Youth, Poor Youth, and
Youth Welfare Recipients

Fix and Zimmermann (2001) also find that mixed-status children are
disproportionately poor at the national level.

Employment of Parents If Co-Resident

Parental employment is important not only for increasing access to
resources but also for helping developing children and youth establish
expectations for "a framework of daily behavior" (Wilson, 1997).
Working parents with employment networks will increase a child's
chances of finding a job when he or she is ready to enter the workforce.

Considerations of work effort by race and generation simultaneously
suggest very different patterns for the parents of Hispanic dependent
youth than for their Asian and white counterparts. Hispanic parents of
higher-generation children are more likely than parents of first-
generation children to be unemployed (although the change from second
to third generation is not statistically significant), whereas the opposite is

true for parents of Asian and white youth (Figure 3.9). Note, however, that there is no difference between the second- and third-generation level of parental unemployment among Hispanic and Asian parents. Differences for whites are not statistically significant. Recall that few Hispanic first-generation youth arriving at ages 10 or older live with their parents.

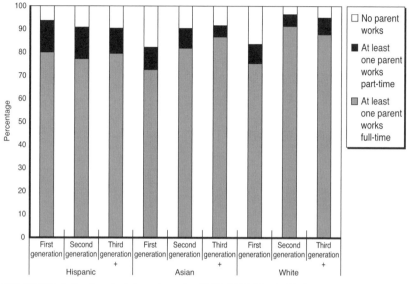

SOURCES: Author's calculations from the 1997–2001 March CPS.

Figure 3.9—Parental Work Effort for Co-Resident California Youth Ages 13 to 24, by Generation and Race/Ethnicity

Educational Attainment of Parents if Co-Resident

Another important indicator of resources available to immigrant youth is the educational attainment of their parents. Variations in educational attainment (Figure 3.10) provide some suggestion of why poverty rates may be so high for Hispanic immigrant youth, despite the considerable work effort of their parents.

Among youth still living with their parent(s), we find that the most educated parent of over half of Hispanic first-generation youth has less

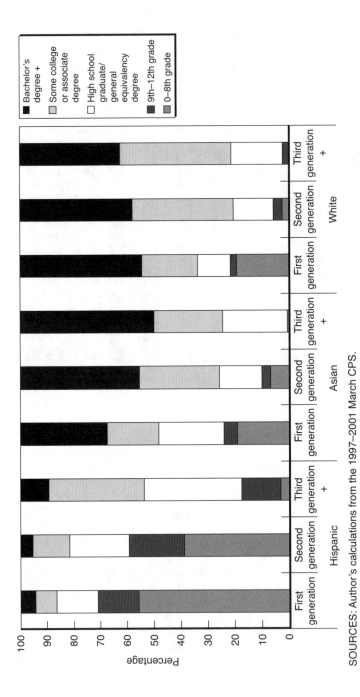

SOURCES: Author's calculations from the 1997–2001 March CPS.

Figure 3.10—Parental Education for Co-Resident California Youth Ages 13 to 24, by Generation and Race/Ethnicity

than a ninth grade education. Fewer than 10 percent have graduated from college. Parents of third-generation Hispanic youth are much more likely than either first- or second-generation parents to have graduated from high school. Each generation of parents of Hispanic youth has lower educational attainment than white or Asian parents. Among whites, parents of third-generation youth are actually less likely than parents of first generation youth to have graduated from college, again illustrating the difficulty in comparing generations in a cross-section. Nearly half of parents of first-generation Asian youth have attended at least some college. By the second and third generation, this share is over 70 percent. These vast differences in educational attainment are probably strongly related to the wide socioeconomic differences documented above, and they may be relevant to the educational attainment of youth as well.

Health and Health Insurance

According to the CPS, few youth are reported to be in fair or poor health (as opposed to good, very good, or excellent health). Youth who are do not vary tremendously by race or ethnicity, ranging from about 3 percent (Asians and whites) to just over 5 percent (blacks). There are no differences in reported health status for immigrant and native-born children in the CPS. However, results from the 2001 California Health Interview Survey find much higher rates of fair and poor health reported for children ages 0 to 17, ranging from 4 percent for Asian children to 15 percent of Hispanic children (Aguayo et al., 2003). Other data point to differences by generation as well. The National Survey of American Families finds that 13 percent of first- and second generation children ages 12 to 17 are in "fair" or "poor" health as reported by their caregivers, whereas the same is true for only 5 percent of third-generation children ages 12 to 17 (Reardon-Anderson, Capps, and Fix, 2002). Using the same data, but for California only, Furstenberg, Waller, and Wang (2003) find that first- and second-generation Hispanic children have worse health than other children yet receive less medical care. Self-rated health measures in the CPS, therefore, appear to be a blunt instrument to measure health among young people, and other research suggests that between-group differences in self-rated health may not reflect actual differences in health. Shetterly et al. (1996) find that Hispanic adults are twice as likely as other racial and ethnic groups to rate their own health as fair or poor, even when controlling for objective health status (reported illnesses, hospitalization, and prescription drug use).

Health insurance coverage, however, does vary a great deal among the racial and ethnic and generation groups of California's youth and is not subject to the same problem of interpretation as is self-rated health status. Hispanic youth are the most likely to report having no health insurance coverage (43%), followed by Asians (28%), blacks (25%), and whites (18%).[5] The state total was 29 percent for youth. Health insurance coverage rates are higher among second and third-generation youth than among first-generation youth for all racial and ethnic groups, (Figure 3.11, which controls for age, as described in footnote 2). The most dramatic changes in coverage rates occurs for Hispanic youth. Sixty-four percent of foreign-born Hispanics who arrive in the United States when age 10 or older lack health insurance coverage, but by the third generation, only 23 percent are without coverage. In the third generation, Hispanic youth are still more likely than whites and Asian third-generation youth to lack health insurance.

Given the availability of publicly provided low-cost health insurance, it is somewhat surprising that so many Hispanic youth are uninsured. However, a recent study of new Hispanic immigrant mothers found that more than half of the study subjects in a large California city were likely to report problems or fears associated with applying for health insurance for their babies (New York Forum for Child Health, 2002). The study's authors attribute these troubles and fears to a "climate of fear" begun after the passage of Proposition 187, and more than one-third of these California Hispanic immigrant mothers reported being worried that they might have to provide a Social Security number to apply for coverage.

---

[5]These percentages for youth are significantly higher than those for California's children ages 0 to 17 by race (Brown et al., 2002) and those for children ages 0 to 17 overall (18%) according to *Kids Count Data Book* (2002).

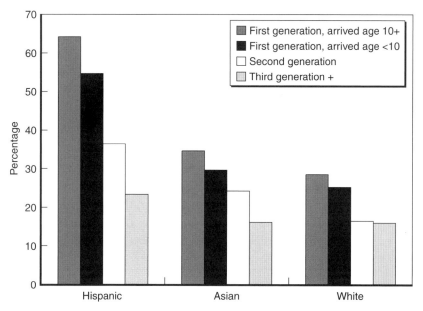

SOURCES: Author's calculations from the 1997–2001 March CPS.
NOTE: Results are age-standardized.

Figure 3.11—Percentage of California Youth Ages 13 to 24 Without Health Insurance, by Generation and Race/Ethnicity

Youth Mortality

The health of Hispanics poses what some in the public health community refer to as an epidemiological paradox (Hayes-Bautista, 2002; Peete, 1999). Despite being more likely to be poor and less educated, Latinos fare as well as whites and better than blacks on a number of health outcomes that appear to be related to socioeconomic status, such as infant mortality, birth weight, rates of mortality from heart disease, cancer, and strokes. Here, rates of external causes of mortality (accidents, homicides, and suicides) are contrasted to internal causes of mortality (disease and congenitally related ailments) by race and

nativity for youth.[6] Although disease and other internal causes of
mortality are responsible for most deaths (93.5% in 2000 and 2001) for
all Californians, externally caused deaths are responsible for the majority
of deaths among youth (72% in 2000 and 2001). Hayes-Bautista (2002)
finds that Hispanics of all ages have higher rates of mortality from
homicide but does not explore differences related to nativity. Sorenson
and Shen (1996) find that Hispanics ages 15 to 34 have lower suicide
rates than whites and blacks, and that the Hispanic foreign-born are less
likely to commit suicide than the Hispanic native-born.

Mortality rates increase with age (Figure 3.12). This is true for both
internal and external causes of mortality, although the rate of increases in
mortality from external causes is much larger than that for internal
causes. Mortality rates of all types are highest among blacks and lowest

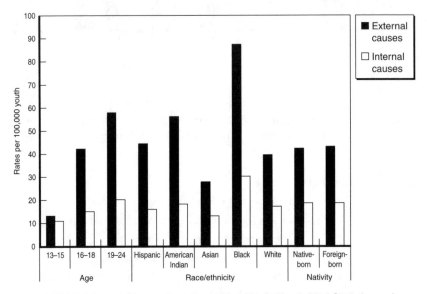

SOURCES: Author's calculations from the 2000–2001 California Vital Statistics and
Census 2000 SF1.

**Figure 3.12—Mortality Rates for California Youth Ages 13 to 24, by Age,
Race/Ethnicity, and Nativity**

[6]In this analysis, we can only separate foreign-born from native-born and cannot
disaggregate the second and third generations. See the appendix for more details.

among Asian youth, and Hispanics and whites appear to have approximately the same mortality rates. This is surprising, given the older age composition of Hispanics. There appear to be no differences by nativity status in rates of mortality from external or internal causes. However, there is a great deal of variation by racial and ethnic groups and age in mortality, and this bears separate analysis.

Up until ages 19 to 24, native-born youth actually have a slight advantage in avoiding mortality from external causes; at ages 19 to 24, the pattern is reversed, with the exception of Asian youth (Figure 3.13). Overall, Asian youth have the lowest rates of externally caused mortality and Hispanic youth the highest.

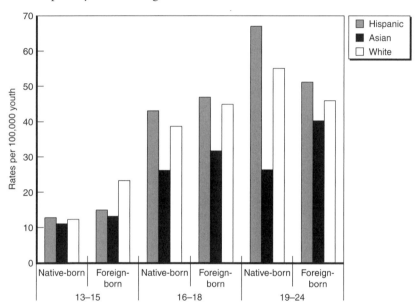

SOURCES: Author's calculations from the 2000–2001 California Vital Statistics and Census 2000 SF1.

Figure 3.13—Mortality Rates from External Causes for California Youth Ages 13 to 24, by Age, Race/Ethnicity, and Nativity

Computer and Telephone Access

Almost all youth live in households with telephones, although there are some noteworthy differences regarding computer access by generation and race. Hispanic youth are the least likely to have computer access in their households, but that access is higher for later generations (Figure 3.14). Overall, white and Asian youth are fairly similar in their levels of access to computers. Third-generation Asian youth are no more likely than first-generation Asian youth to be without home computer access, although sample sizes are extremely small.

This chapter has demonstrated that there are clear and large differences between immigrant and native-born youth on a number of resources measures. Resource levels are not uniform by generation, however, and seem to be related both to age at arrival and race and ethnicity. For example, immigrants who arrive before age 10 are likely to live with their own parents or other relatives at rates closer to those of their native-born counterparts than at the rates of later-arriving immigrant youth within each racial and ethnic group. Within the group of immigrant youth who arrive at age 10 or older, Hispanic immigrants are much more likely than Asian immigrants to live on their own or to

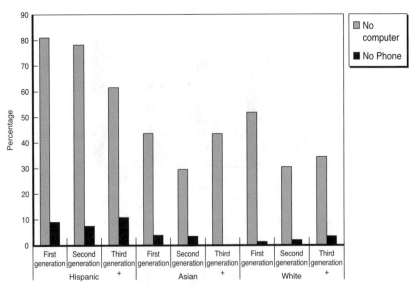

SOURCES: Author's calculations from the 1997 October CPS.

Figure 3.14—Computer and Telephone Access for California Youth Ages 13 to 24, by Generation and Race/Ethnicity

36

have started their own families. These household and family relationships appear to bear a strong relationship to measures of resources, such as poverty levels. Similarly, more than half of Hispanic immigrant youth arriving at age 10 or older lack health insurance. Rates of health insurance coverage for late-arriving Asian immigrant youth are also higher than for those who arrive before age 10, but the overall percentage of these youth who lack coverage is much lower—closer to 30 percent. Finally, differences in resources still persist among today's third generation youth. Third-generation Hispanic and Asian youth are more likely than white youth to be poor, and Hispanic youth are significantly more likely than either Asian or white youth to lack health insurance and to have started families.

4. What Are California's Youth Doing?

The previous chapter illustrated the large gaps that exist between immigrant youth and natives in resource levels (poverty, health insurance, parental education, etc.). Those gaps suggest that the investments Californians make in youth may not be reaching immigrant youth at sufficient levels. The eventual well-being of immigrant youth may be more important, however, than their current resource levels. By investigating the activities in which immigrant youth are currently involved and comparing them across racial and ethnic groups and to the native-born, Californians and policymakers can assess whether it seems likely that immigrant youth will eventually make progress in closing these gaps in their own lifetimes or in those of their children.

This chapter provides a portrait of the complex balances many of today's youth, especially immigrant youth, are striking between school, work, and family. It begins by describing the mix of activities in which youth are involved—school, work, and parenting—and then examines each in turn. A small number of youth are not engaged in any of these activities. These youth are described, as are the reasons they give for their inactivity. Readers should note that this report considers only the years 1997–2001, a period of strong economic growth nationally and in California. The chapter concludes with a description of voting behavior (a measure of civic engagement) of California's young adults.

Mix of Activities for Those Age 16 and Older

This section classifies youth activities into mutually exclusive categories: school, work, school and work, parenting only, and inactive. If a young person is participating in school, work (during the previous 12 months), or school and work, he or she is coded into the relevant category, even if he or she is also parenting. If a young person was neither in school nor working but was living with his or her child, we categorized that youth as parenting only. Thus, the percentages of youth "parenting only" are not the full percentages of youth who are parenting. These youth will be described below. Youth not participating in school, work, or parenting were classified as inactive. The sample is restricted to those age 16 and older because concurrent employment and enrollment questions were asked only of adults over the age of 15.[1]

School enrollment decreases by age—an increasing share of young people move from the world of school to the world of school and work. The sum of school only and school and work declines from nearly 90 percent at ages 16 to 18 to approximately 40 percent for ages 19 to 24 (Figure 4.1). The majority of the younger youth group is engaged only in school, but nearly half of the older youth group is engaged only in work. The percentage of young women whose sole activity is parenting increases four times, from 2 percent to 8 percent by ages 19 to 24. Inactivity also increases with age for both sexes.

Because almost all youth ages 13 to 18 are in school, the next two figures illustrate activities by sex, race, and generation for youth ages 19 to 24. The first examines activities for young women (Figure 4.2). Among women, Hispanics are the most likely to be parenting only, especially first-generation women who arrived between the ages of 10 and 17 and at age 18 and older. Lack of measurable activity is higher among first generation Hispanics and Asians than among subsequent generations, although differences between whites and Asians by generation are slight. Second-generation Hispanic young women are more likely than those in the first generation to be attending school. Asian and white young women exhibit the opposite pattern. Third-generation Asian and white young women are actually less likely than first-generation Asian and white youth to be involved in school. This

---

[1]This analysis is based on just one cross-section—the years 1997–2001. Research that examines multiple time periods always finds that the proportions of adults participating in school and work vary according to economic conditions. Generally, when unemployment is high, fewer adults work, more adults are in school, and more adults are inactive. Thus, comparisons made between the findings in this report to research covering differing time periods may demonstrate different results for the rates of participation in the labor force, schooling, parenting, and inactivity.

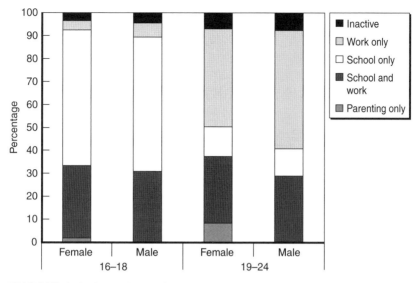

SOURCES: Author's calculations from the 1997–2001 March CPS.

Figure 4.1—Activities of California Youth Ages 16 to 24, by Age and Sex

may be a sign of "negative" or "downward" assimilation such as was found among children of Asian immigrants with increasing time in the United States (Portes and Rumbaut, 2001), or it could be caused by comparing generations that are not uniform in ancestry or background, such as parental educational attainment, even within racial groups. Asian and white young women are more likely to be working without attending school in later generations.

Hispanic men ages 19 to 24 are very involved in work. This is especially true of first-generation Hispanics youth who arrive between the ages of 10 and 17 and at age 18 and older. Nearly 80 percent work alone (Figure 4.3). Among Hispanics, inactivity is nearly constant across generations, although there does not appear to be a tremendous variation among any of the groups. First-generation Hispanic young men who arrived in the United States before age 10 are almost as involved in school as second-generation Hispanic youth. Each generation has significantly higher school enrollment than the first-generation youth who arrived after age 10. However, levels are lower in the third

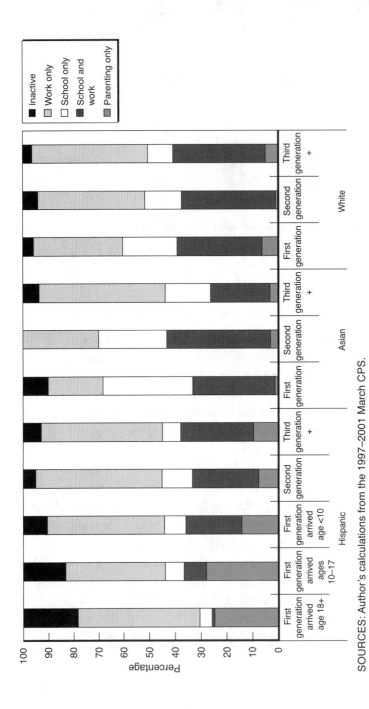

SOURCES: Author's calculations from the 1997–2001 March CPS.

Figure 4.2—Activities of California Young Women Ages 19 to 24, by Generation and Race/Ethnicity

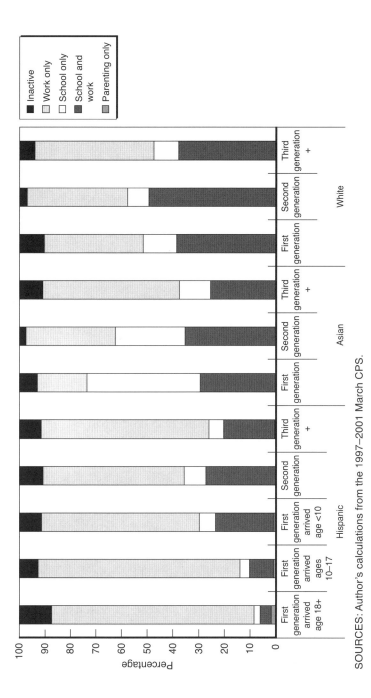

SOURCES: Author's calculations from the 1997–2001 March CPS.

Figure 4.3—Activities of California Young Men Ages 19 to 24, by Generation and Race/Ethnicity

generation than in the second, although this difference is not statistically significant. Other research also found no real differences in educational attainment between the second and third generation for adult Hispanics (Grogger and Trejo, 2002), whereas research using repeated cross-sections (Smith, 2003) has demonstrated progress between and second- and third-generation Hispanics.

Nearly 75 percent of first generation Asian youth ages 19 to 24 are in school, suggesting that some may have migrated to the United States to attend university. Because of small samples in the CPS, their activities cannot be disaggregated by age at arrival. By the third generation, only 37 percent of Asian young men are in school. Differences among whites by generation are small. Among third-generation youth, significant differences in school participation exist: 26 percent of Hispanics, 37 percent of Asians, and 48 percent of whites are in school. Note that almost none of these young men are involved in parenting only.

School Enrollment

Nationally, Hispanic youth have the highest high school dropout rates; each year approximately 7 percent drop out (Jamieson, Curry, and Martinez, 2001). A larger share of Hispanic youth than youth of any other racial or ethnic group has neither finished high school nor is enrolled in school. Educational enrollment is of particular concern for Hispanic immigrant youth because, unlike white and Asian youth, the foreign-born have lower scholastic achievement than do the native-born (Vernez and Mizell, 2001). However, other research has found that first- and second-generation youth are actually less likely than third-generation Hispanic youth to drop out of high school once such variables as school performance and family background characteristics are held constant (Driscoll, 1999).

Figures 4.2 and 4.3 pointed to these differences in current enrollment among Hispanic youth ages 19 to 24. Low enrollment levels do not necessarily describe conditions or the quality of the education immigrant youth receive. This section investigates differences by generation and race and ethnicity in college enrollment. Jamieson et al. (2001) suggest that part-time enrollment is most often a school-going strategy used by the poor; thus, a greater share of minority and immigrant college students might attend part-time. Part-time attendance is also associated with lower graduation rates (Fry, 2002). Similarly, the community college system (here represented by two-year schools) is both more affordable and more accommodating of part-time schedules, so its use might vary by generation as well. However, if families begin sending their youth to college at higher rates as generation increases, more youth may use the community college system.

Hispanic college students are more likely than white or Asian students to attend part-time, but in later generations, more attend full-time (Figure 4.4). Asian and white youth, although less likely to attend part-time than Hispanic students, are more likely to attend part-time in the third generation than in the second, although this result is not statistically significant. Among those enrolled in college, Hispanic students are always the most likely of all racial and ethnic groups to attend a two-year college (in excess of 60 percent), regardless of

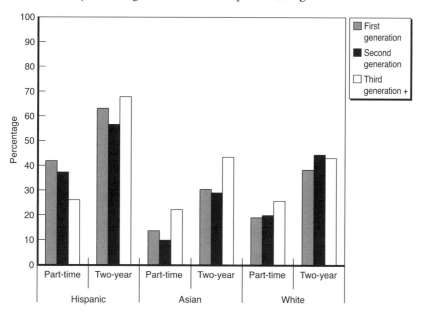

SOURCES: Author's calculations from the 1997–2001 October CPS.

Figure 4.4—Part-Time and Two-Year College Attendance for California College Students Ages 19 to 24, by Generation and Race/Ethnicity

generation. Given that two-year colleges are already the most frequently used institutions of higher education among Hispanics, they are important institutions to use in efforts to increase Hispanic educational attainment. Because of smaller sample sizes of college students, it is not possible to examine type of enrollment by age at arrival among the first generation.

Educational Attainment

Understanding variations in school enrollment and college attendance patterns is important, but because schooling is an ongoing investment for many youth, it does not tell us much about eventual outcomes. This section describes educational attainment among all youth ages 19 to 24. The focus is on older ages because most of those who will obtain high school diplomas will have done so by age 19 and, many of those who will enroll in college will have done so by age 19 or 20.

Overall, Hispanics are the least educated and Asian youth are the most. Over 75 percent of Asian youth have at least some college education; the same is true for only about 30 percent of Hispanic youth. Furthermore, nearly 40 percent of Hispanic youth at these ages did not complete high school. Despite a sizable Asian immigrant population, virtually no Asian youth have less than a ninth grade education.

Given that many foreign-born youth are likely to face financial constraints, it would not be surprising to find that they have relatively low levels of educational attainment. However, it is primarily Hispanic immigrants who have low levels of education, particularly those who arrived after age 10. Over 40 percent of Hispanic immigrants ages 19 to 24 who arrived in the United States after age 17 have less than a ninth grade education, and approximately 30 percent have only some high school education (Figure 4.5). Whereas the percentage of Hispanics who have less than a ninth grade education is lower for those who arrived between the ages of 10 and 17 (28%), it is lower still for those who arrived by age 10 (7%). Gonzalez (2003) found similar patterns among immigrant Hispanic adults—the younger the age at arrival, the greater the number of years of school completed. Very few second- and third-generation youth (2% and 1%, respectively) have less than a ninth grade

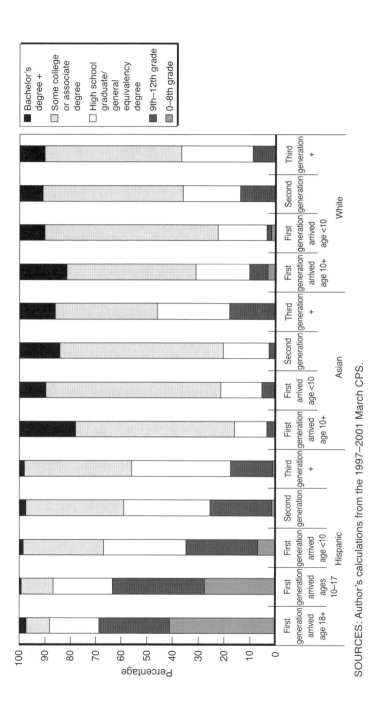

Legend:
- Bachelor's degree +
- Some college or associate degree
- High school graduate/ general equivalency degree
- 9th–12th grade
- 0–8th grade

SOURCES: Author's calculations from the 1997–2001 March CPS.

Figure 4.5—Educational Attainment of California Youth Ages 19 to 24, by Generation and Race/Ethnicity

education. This may suggest that some Hispanic second-generation youth spend some of their childhood in their parent's countries of origin. Indeed, there are accounts of foreign-born parents sending their U.S.-raised children home to be educated or raised with the "proper authority" by grandparents or other relatives (Portes and Rumbaut, 2001).

In contrast, Asian immigrant youth who arrived in the United States after age 10 have the highest levels of educational attainment of any youth, even higher than third-generation Asians. Twenty-two percent have already earned four-year degrees and an additional 62 percent have attended at least some college. None have less than a ninth grade education, and only 3 percent have less than a high school diploma. Some of these 19 to 24 year old Asian immigrant youth likely came to the United States to attend college. Fry (2002) finds that about half of the F-1 student visas in 1999 went to Asians, whereas only 15 percent went to Hispanics. Approximately 80 percent of both first- and second-generation Asian youth have at least some college education. Educational attainment is considerably lower for third-generation Asian youth: Only 54 percent have at least some college. Among whites, the first generation is also the most educated. Although successive generations of Hispanic youth have better educational outcomes relative to the current first generation, this pattern does not appear to hold for Asian and white youth. The third-generation whites and Asians are considerably better educated than are Hispanics, 44 percent of whom have attended at least some college (versus 54% of Asians and 63% of whites).

Work

This section considers the proportion of youth working (over the course of the last year), and examines their work effort. Work effort is defined as full-time if it was at least 35 weeks a year, and during those weeks, at least 35 hours. Part-time labor is any amount of work less than full-time. The population of workers does not include those looking for work.

At younger ages (15 to 18), only about 15 percent of Hispanic, Asian, and black youth work. The vast majority of that employment is part-time or part-year. Over one-quarter of white youth ages 15 to 18 work (results not shown). Research focusing on immigrant children (under age 18) and combining all racial and ethnic groups finds that children of immigrants are actually less likely to work than children of natives (Reardon-Anderson, Capps, and Fix, 2002). Older immigrant youth, however, appear to be more invested in work than are natives. Hispanic young men ages 19 to 24 are heavily invested in work—over 80 percent of each generation works, with little change among the generations (Figure 4.6).[2] However, Asian and white first-generation youth are less likely to work than their second- and third-generation counterparts.

The share of Hispanic youth working full-time is lower in the third generation than in any of the previous generations and is replaced by part-time work. Among Asian and white young men, total work effort is higher in the third generation than in the first, but for Asian youth, a much greater share work part-time rather than full-time. Results for young women (not shown) indicate that work effort is higher in later generations, mostly through increases in full-time work.

Marriage, Births, and Parenting Among Youth

Chapter 3 illustrated that many youth, especially Hispanic immigrant youth, have started their own families or households. Of those youth, 59 percent are married, 5 percent were previously married or are separated, and the remainder have never married.[3] Two-thirds of youth who are family heads (or spouses) have children. Marital status for parenting youth is almost identical to that for youth who are heading their own families: Over half of these parents are married (56%), 7 percent are either previously married or separated, and 37 percent have never been married.

Two measures capture family formation at young ages. Rates of births to teens (ages 15 to 19) in California are examined first using vital

---

[2]These figures exclude students.

[3]Note that the unit of analysis here is the individual rather than the couple. Thus, in cases where both members of a couple fall into the youth age range of ages 13 to 24, both are counted in our estimates of percentage married. However, most married youth in our sample (approximately two-thirds) are partnered with spouses age 25 or older.

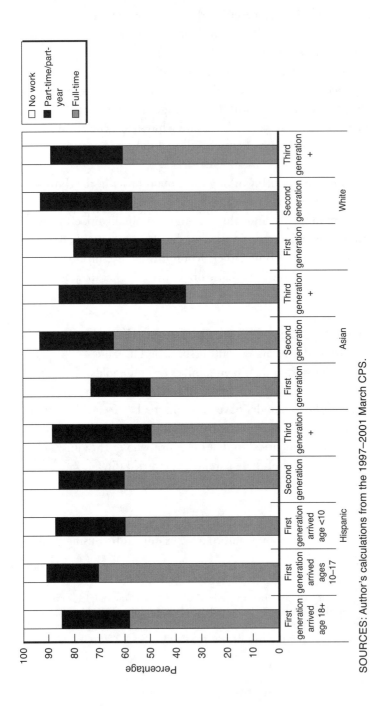

SOURCES: Author's calculations from the 1997–2001 March CPS.

Figure 4.6—Work Effort of California Young Men Ages 19 to 24 Not Attending School, by Generation and Race/Ethnicity

statistics. Second, the share of young women who are parenting and their activities are described. Rich detail in the CPS permits the description of circumstances of family formation, but a more accurate measure of the occurrence of teen parenthood is available in California birth certificate data.

Teen birth rates (the number of births per thousand girls ages 15 to 19) are important because of their correlation with poverty of the teen mother and child. Teen mothers are rarely married at the time of birth (24% in 1999, according to Johnson, 2003), often will not earn a high school diploma, and may have a more difficult time providing for the emotional needs of their children. In 2000, foreign-born Hispanic teens had fertility rates nearly twice as high as those for native-born Hispanics (Figure 4.7). On average, Hispanic teen fertility rates are much higher than those for the other racial groups. White and black foreign-born youth have lower fertility rates than those of the native-born. Asian teen girls have nearly equal fertility rates whether they are native- or foreign-

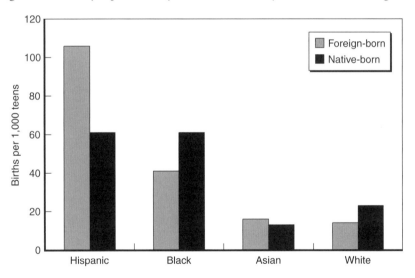

SOURCE: Johnson (2003).

Figure 4.7—Teen Birth Rates for California Young Women Ages 15 to 19, by Race/Ethnicity and Nativity, 2000

born. Foreign-born teen mothers, however, are much more likely than native-born teen mothers to be married (Johnson, 2003). Among the native-born, Hispanics and blacks have similar rates of teenage childbearing, which are approximately three times as high as those for white and Asian teens.

Fertility rates tell us only about births to young people. To examine the complex work, school, and home arrangements young parents make, the CPS data are explored. In the CPS, parenting is ascertained through maternal and child co-residence. Mothers who are not residing with their children are not considered in this analysis, and this likely causes an underestimate of mothers but not of active parents.[4]

Because Hispanics are the ethnic group most likely to be parenting as youth and because of their large sample in the CPS, their parenting activities can be examined by generation. About 19 percent of first-generation Hispanic 16 to 18 year olds who arrived after age 10 are mothers (Table 4.1). The percentage parenting is lower (10%) for those who arrived by age 10 and lower still for native-born Hispanic youth women ages 16 to 18. Many Hispanic young women ages 19 to 24 are

Table 4.1

Percentage of California Hispanic Young Women Parenting, by Generation and Age

Generation	16 to 18	19 to 24
First, arrived age 18+	—	44
First, arrived ages 10–17	19	48
First, arrived age <10	10	31
Second	5	32
Third +	7	40

SOURCES: Author's calculations from the 1997–2001 March CPS.

---

[4]Numbers of youth-aged fathers residing with their children is so small that fathers were excluded from this analysis. Fathers rarely appear in this data for two reasons: (1) Younger parents are less likely than older parents to be married or cohabiting, and children are more likely to live with their mothers than with their fathers, and (2) some young mothers may be partnered with men over the age of 25 who do not appear in this analysis.

already parents. Over 40 percent of the foreign-born who arrived after age 17 are mothers as are nearly half of those who arrived between the ages of 10 and 17. Approximately one-third of those who arrived before age 10 as well as one-third of the second generation are parenting. Motherhood rates are higher among the third generation than among the second, which is similar to what Hill and Johnson (2002) found among all Hispanic women ages 15 to 44.

First-generation Hispanic mothers ages 19 to 24 are most likely of all generations to stay at home with their children (Figure 4.8). For the mothers who engage in an activity outside of the home, the most common activity is work, regardless of generation. Almost none of Hispanic mothers who arrived in the United States at age 10 or older are in school. For those who arrived before age 10, 8 percent are either in school or in school and working, and this percentage is only somewhat higher among second- and third-generation Hispanic mothers.

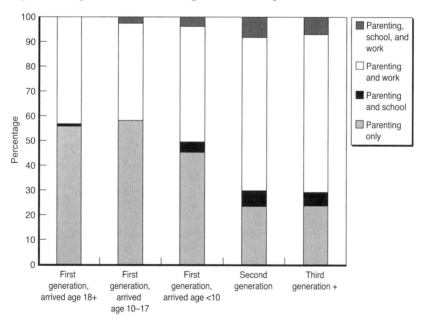

SOURCES: Author's calculations from the 1997–2001 March CPS.

Figure 4.8—Activities of California Parenting Hispanic Young Women Ages 19 to 24, by Generation

Lack of Measurable Activity

This section examines in closer detail youth who are not measurably working, in school, or parenting in the previous year, whom we term "inactive." This measure of inactivity may include those who are looking for work. Research based on a national survey of youth finds that Hispanic youth have relatively high levels of inactivity, but that by later youth ages, those rates fall bellow those of whites and blacks (Powers, 1994). National longitudinal surveys rarely have sufficient numbers of Asian youth with which to perform a comparable analysis.

Approximately 6 percent of youth ages 16 to 24 are inactive. This number is somewhat lower than in other research because of the way we have defined "inactive" here (not in school, no work during the previous year, and not currently parenting). Recall from Figures 4.2 and 4.3 that Hispanic youth are slightly more likely than other youth to be inactive.

Because few youth are inactive, it is difficult to do much detailed analysis by race and generation. Only the case of inactive Hispanic youth can reasonably be examined using the CPS sample. The most common reasons for not working among the inactive are an inability to find work and being retired (Figure 4.9). The percentage stating "retired" appears to decline by generation, suggesting that perhaps it is related to language comprehension. More than 20 percent of first-generation youth state that they are "retired" compared to 10 percent of third-generation youth. Foreign-born Hispanic youth may not understand that being "retired" implies never returning to the world of work. Also notable is the higher percentage of self-reports of being ill as a reason for not working across generations, although these differences are not statistically significant.

Citizenship and Voting

Another measure of youth activity available for California youth is civic participation as measured by citizenship and voting (among those age 18 and older). Other measures, such as participation in volunteer organizations, church, and school extracurricular activities, would be desirable but do not exist at the state level by immigrant generation.

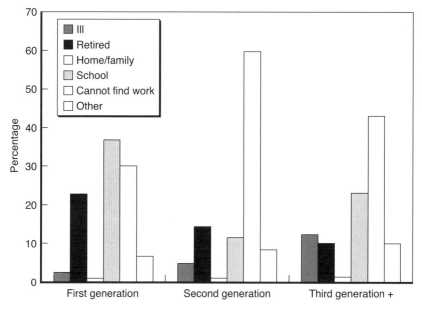

SOURCES: Author's calculations from the 1997–2001 March CPS.

Figure 4.9—Reasons for Not Working Given by Inactive California Hispanic Youth Ages 16 to 24, by Generation

First-generation youth have very low participation rates in the electoral process, but this is mostly because of lack of citizenship (Table 4.2). Participation rates vary to some extent by race because Asian and white first-generation youth are more likely than Hispanic-first generation youth to be eligible to vote.

Among the eligible population, registration rates by generation range from approximately 10 percent to somewhat more than half. There is no pattern as generation increases. In some cases, the first generation who arrived before age 10 and second generations have lower registration among the eligible than the first. However, there are clear differences by racial and ethnic groups. Hispanics and blacks are almost always the least likely to register and whites and Asians are the most likely.

Table 4.2
Political Participation of California Youth Ages 18 to 24

	Race/Ethnicity	% Citizen	% Registered	% of Citizens Who Registered	% Who Voted	% Registered Who Voted	Total Number
First generation, arrived age 10+	Hispanic	5.3	0.5	9.8	0.2	43.7	281
	Asian	20.1	8.4	41.5	5.3	63.3	95
	White	24.5	16.1	66.0	10.3	63.7	44
First generation, arrived age <10	Hispanic	21.7	6.0	27.7	5.4	90.1	134
	Asian	53.3	16.5	30.9	9.3	56.3	75
	White	63.1	22.8	36.1	10.9	47.7	27
Second generation	Hispanic	100.0	36.2	36.2	24.4	67.3	280
	Asian	100.0	32.2	32.2	25.4	78.9	85
	White	100.0	61.5	61.5	42.9	69.8	84
Third generation +	Hispanic	100.0	44.0	44.0	32.4	73.7	149
	Asian	100.0	78.2	78.2	66.0	84.3	26
	Black	100.0	41.4	41.4	29.7	71.8	104
	White	100.0	49.2	49.2	35.3	71.8	608
Grand total		75.7	33.9	44.8	24.2	71.3	1,992

SOURCES: Author's calculations from the 1998 and 2000 November CPS.

Among second-generation youth, Asians and Hispanics vote at same rate: approximately one-quarter.[5] White second-generation youth are more likely to vote—over 40 percent do so. This difference is also reflected in higher registration rates among second generation whites. In the third generation, Hispanic and white youth vote at roughly the same rate—approximately one-third. Asian third-generation youth are much more likely to vote—two-thirds do so, but very few third-generation Asians answer voting questions on the CPS. Controlling for registration, voting is higher by generation. Differences in voting by race are small in the third generation—all groups range from approximately 70 to 85 percent.

Despite the differences in resource levels highlighted in Chapter 3, it appears that some immigrant youth may have a brighter future ahead. This is especially true for early-arriving immigrant youth who appear to attend school at the same rates as their native-born counterparts and who are significantly less likely than late-arriving immigrant youth to begin parenting at young ages. Asian late-arriving immigrant youth are investing heavily in schooling (sometimes more than their native-born counterparts). Their future outlook is good. Hispanic immigrant youth arriving after age 10, however, are not enrolling in schools at rates that are promising for their futures or those of their children. They are heavily invested in the world of work, but earlier results, such as those for poverty rates, suggest that they are not earning enough to provide adequately for themselves or their families. For many of these youth, it appears that schools are not the place to reach them—they have either dropped out or never entered them to begin with. The challenges presented in reaching this group will receive more attention in the concluding chapter.

---

[5]We find that rates of voting among youth are much lower than those found for the adult population of California in Citrin and Highton (2002).

5. How Do Outcomes for Immigrant Youth Vary by Region?

Earlier chapters of this report documented variation in family and individual outcomes and activities for California's immigrant and native youth. This chapter focuses on many of these same outcomes but examines their variation at the regional level to help policymakers identify the areas of greatest need. Table A.2 defines the nine California regions used in this report. Because the Current Population Survey does not interview families in every county of the state, this report cannot precisely replicate the regional definitions used in other PPIC reports (Johnson, 2002), and some important deviations are noted in the table. Because many regions have relatively small sample sizes of youth, age, race, and generation cannot be disaggregated simultaneously. Findings in this chapter follow the same order as the report overall. The first section describes the racial and ethnic distribution of the regions as well as the generational distributions of the regions. English language ability by region is considered in the following section. The next section addresses resource levels of youth at the regional level. The final section considers youth's activities, with an emphasis on education at the regional level.

Racial and Ethnic and Generation Distribution in the State's Regions

White youth predominate in the Central Coast and Sacramento Metro areas (Figure 5.1). Hispanic youth appear in large proportion in Los Angeles County (54%), the San Joaquin Valley, the Inland Empire, the Central Coast, Orange County, and the San Diego regions. Asian

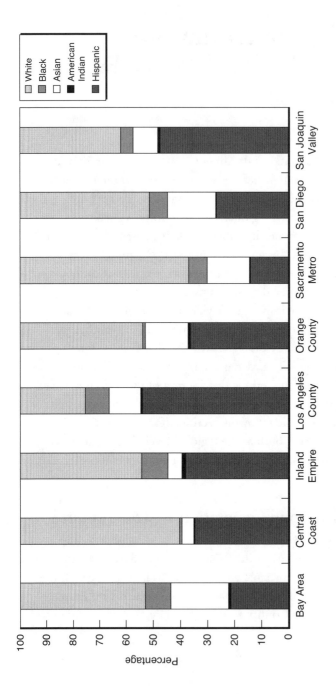

SOURCES: Author's calculations from the 1997–2001 March CPS.

Figure 5.1—Racial/Ethnic Distribution of California Youth Ages 13 to 24 in Eight California Regions

youth are most represented in the Bay Area, Sacramento region, San Diego, and Orange County.

Youth in the Central Coast region are the most likely to be first generation, arriving between the ages of 19 and 24 (9%, Figure 5.2). In total, of all the state's regions, the Central Coast, Los Angeles County, and Orange County have the largest share of first-generation youth who arrived in the United States after age 10 (although the differences are small). Unlike Los Angeles County, the Central Coast has a majority third-generation population. Most regions with a large population of foreign-born youth also have a fairly large population of second-generation youth and, consequently, a third generation, that makes up less than half of the youth population. This may suggest that the Central Coast is a relatively new receiving area for immigrant youth or that families in later generations leave the Central Coast. Overall, Los Angeles and Orange Counties have the highest proportion of first-generation youth (approximately one-third) and the Inland Empire and Sacramento regions have the highest proportion of third-generation youth (in excess of two-thirds).

Regional Differences in Language

Youth in the Central Coast are least likely of all youth to be fluent in English (less than 80% are—see Figure 5.3). Even Los Angeles, which has the same share of youth as the Central Coast arriving after age 10, has English fluency levels closer to 90 percent. Spanish is much more likely to be the only language spoken in households for San Joaquin Valley, Los Angeles County, and Central Coast youth (close to 15%) than for any of the state's other regions.

California's school data provide rich detail about school-going immigrant youth: both where they live and some indication of how they are faring. This section describes students who are learning English in the state, reports on the share of students who are recently arrived immigrants to the United States, and documents the share of students who are classified as members of migrant worker families.

Language ability of students varies by region. Tafoya (2002) provides trends over time for students in grades K–12. Statewide, two-thirds of high school students in public schools are native English

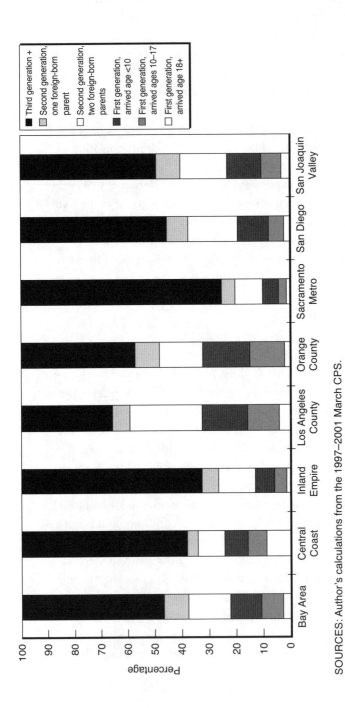

SOURCES: Author's calculations from the 1997–2001 March CPS.

Figure 5.2—Generational Distribution of California Youth Ages 13 to 24 in Eight California Regions

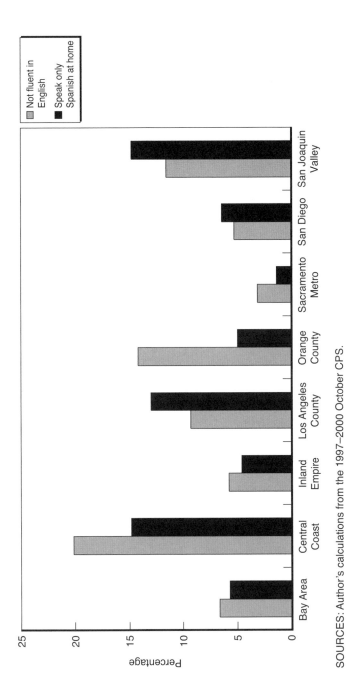

SOURCES: Author's calculations from the 1997–2000 October CPS.

Figure 5.3—Percentage of California Youth Ages 13 to 24 Not Speaking English Fluently and Speaking Only Spanish at Home, by Region

speakers (Table 5.1). Nearly 20 percent are nonnative but fluent English proficient (FEP). The remainder, nearly 16 percent, are classified as English learners (EL). Being a nonnative English speaker is not necessarily a risk factor for poor school performance. Portes and Rumbaut (1996) find that students classified as FEP often have higher grade point averages than those who speak English only. This is true for East Asian, Indochinese, and Filipino students, although it is less clear for Hispanic students. Of those high school students who are EL, over three-quarters are Spanish speakers, less than 20 percent speak an Asian language, and the remaining 5 percent speak another language.[1]

There is a great deal of regional variation in English language proficiency among public high school students.[2] Nearly 96 percent of students in the Sierras are native English speakers, whereas in Los Angeles County, slightly fewer than half of students are. The lowest share of the state's native English speakers is found in Los Angeles County. Orange County has the next lowest percentage of native English speakers among its high school students—60 percent.

Statewide, nearly 16 percent of public high school students are EL. Three of the state's 10 regions appear to have a significantly higher share of EL students: Orange County, Los Angeles County, and the Central Coast. Spanish speakers dominate in these counties. In fact, the percentage of high school students who are Spanish-speaking EL is highest in the Central Coast (17.5%), where nearly one in five high school students is limited English proficient. In general, Spanish-speaking students are more represented than Asian students among English learners (which is not surprising given the size of the Mexican immigrant population relative to the population of immigrants from Asian countries). However, in the Sacramento Metro region, there are actually more Asian EL students than Spanish EL students (the same is true of the Sacramento Metro region's FEP population). Three other

---

[1]CPS data indicate that 95 percent of youth who were reported to not speak English fluently spoke Spanish; the 2000 Census found that percentage to be 90 (see Chapter 2). The CPS is likely to undercount Asian language and "other" language speakers who do not speak English fluently. Designations into FEP and EL also consider writing and reading ability.

[2]See the appendix for detail.

Table 5.1

Language Proficiency of California Students, by Region, 2000–2001, Grades 9–12

	% Native English	% Fluent English Proficient				% English Learner				EL/FEP	Number EL + FEP
		Total	Spanish	Asian	Other	Total	Spanish	Asian	Other		
Statewide	66.1	18.2	11.6	5.0	1.6	15.7	12.2	2.7	0.8	0.9	578,947
Far North	89.4	4.7	3.0	1.6	0.2	5.9	3.9	1.8	0.2	1.2	7,099
Sacramento Metro	82.0	7.1	2.4	3.5	1.1	10.9	4.2	4.9	1.8	1.5	17,677
Sierras	95.5	2.0	1.7	0.1	0.2	2.6	2.1	0.4	0.1	1.3	466
Bay Area	70.9	16.2	5.5	8.5	2.2	12.9	7.6	4.3	1.0	0.8	82,473
San Joaquin Valley	68.3	15.8	11.4	3.5	0.9	15.9	11.9	3.6	0.5	1.0	66,633
Central Coast	69.7	11.9	10.5	1.0	0.3	18.4	17.5	0.7	0.2	1.5	20,539
Inland Empire	76.4	10.4	8.7	1.3	0.5	13.1	11.8	0.9	0.4	1.3	46,041
L.A. County	48.9	31.5	22.1	6.5	2.9	19.5	16.1	2.4	1.1	0.6	228,037
Orange County	60.0	18.1	9.1	7.1	2.0	21.9	17.1	3.9	0.9	1.2	56,304
San Diego	69.2	16.2	10.7	4.4	1.1	14.6	12.7	1.2	0.7	0.9	46,036

SOURCE: Author's calculations from 2000–2001 Language Census, California Department of Education.

regions, have a significant proportion of Asian EL students: the Bay Area, Orange County, and the San Joaquin Valley, although nowhere in the state is the proportion greater than 8.5 percent of the high school student population.

Regions with a high share of FEP students may have been very successful in teaching students English or may have an immigrant student population that enters the system while young (or with a high degree of English proficiency). Statewide, slightly more than half of the nonnative English speakers are classified as FEP (18%) versus EL (16%). However, a much larger share of nonnative English speakers in the Central Coast and the Sacramento regions are classified as EL rather than FEP. In the both the Central Coast and the Sacramento region, the EL share is 1.5 times as large as the FEP share. In the Far North and Inland Empire, the EL share is 1.25 times the size of the FEP share. Although Los Angeles County has the greatest percentage of nonnative speakers, the majority are FEP rather than EL. The same is true in the Bay Area.

Regional Differences in Resources

Chapter 3 documented variations in resources among immigrant youth by race and ethnicity and generation. Hispanic first-generation youth fared poorly relative to Asian and white first-generation youth, especially those who arrived in the United States after age 10. Because sample sizes are small at the regional level, we examine resources overall and, where possible, by generation or race and ethnicity.

Welfare receipt is highest among youth residing in San Joaquin Valley and lowest among those living in the Bay Area, Central Coast, and Orange County (Figure 5.4). Low welfare receipt among Central Coast families may be due to high degrees of ineligibility—indeed, poverty levels are quite similar to those in the San Joaquin Valley, yet rates of public assistance in youth households are much lower. In fact, the Central Coast and the Bay Area have similar public assistance rates (about 4%), but poverty is more than twice as prevalent in the Central Coast than in the Bay Area. In addition, youth in the Central Coast

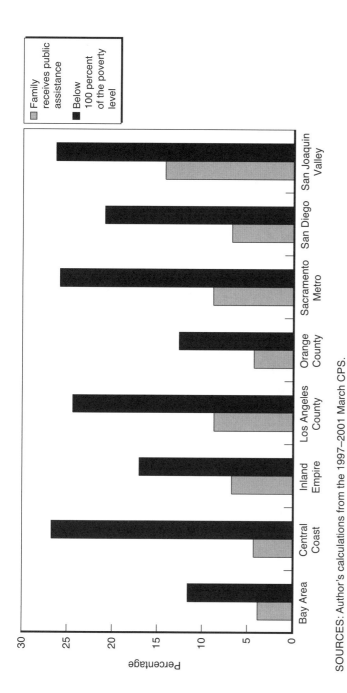

SOURCES: Author's calculations from the 1997–2001 March CPS.

NOTE: Results are not age-adjusted.

Figure 5.4—Resources Among California Youth Ages 13 to 24, by Region

region are the most likely not to have a telephone in their households. Sacramento Metro youth are most likely to have telephones, but there is little variation by region on this dimension (the range is from 3% to 9%). Household computer access also varies little (not shown).

Because Hispanic youth are both the most likely to be members of noncitizen families and have the largest samples sizes in the CPS, we examine family citizenship status by region for them. We see a great deal of regional variation in the percentage of Hispanic youth who live in noncitizen families (Figure 5.5). In the Central Coast and Orange County, more than one-third of Hispanic youth live in noncitizen families, meaning that no member, child or adult, is a citizen.

Health insurance coverage rates are markedly worse in Los Angeles County than in the state's other regions, and the Bay Area has rates of health insurance coverage that are significantly higher than those in the other regions (Table 5.2). Over half of Hispanic youth in the Central Coast and Orange County lack insurance coverage. Hispanic youth in Los Angeles County face similarly low rates of health insurance coverage (48%). Statewide, 43 percent of Hispanic youth and 29 percent of all youth are uninsured.

Regional Variations in Youth Activities

At ages 13 to 15, virtually all children are enrolled in school. Among first-generation youth ages 16 to 24, however, those in the Central Coast are the least likely to be enrolled in school. Nearly 80 percent are not in school (Table 5.3). School enrollment for immigrant youth is lower than for the native-born. Here, enrollment rates for first-generation youth are compared across regions. Because of small sample sizes, enrollment rates cannot be simultaneously displayed for generation and race/ethnicity. Only in the Bay Area are more than half of immigrants ages 16 to 24 enrolled in school. The San Joaquin Valley stands out in its low enrollment rates among all youth, not just immigrants. Regardless of generation, somewhere around half of all youth ages 16 to 24 are not in school.

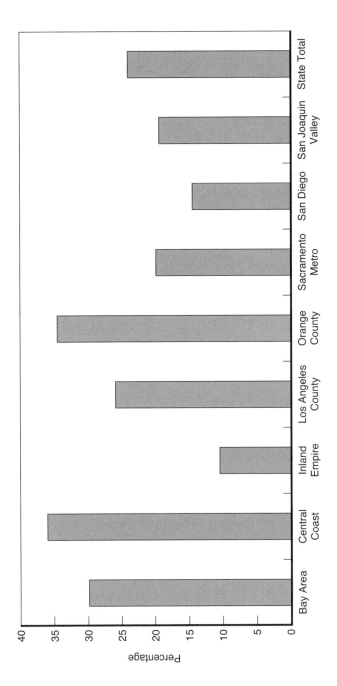

SOURCES: Author's calculations from the 1997–2001 March CPS.

Figure 5.5—Percentage of California Hispanic Youth Ages 13 to 24 in Noncitizen Families, by Region

Table 5.2

**Percentage of California Youth Ages 13 to 24
Uninsured, by Region: Total and Hispanic**

Region	Total	Hispanic
Bay Area	22	35
Central Coast	27	53
Inland Empire	25	35
Los Angeles County	39	48
Orange County	30	54
Sacramento Metro	22	34
San Diego	29	42
San Joaquin Valley	25	33
State Total	29	43

SOURCES: Author's calculations from the
1997–2001 March CPS.

NOTE: Results are not age-adjusted.

Table 5.3

**Percentage of California Youth Ages 16 to 24 Not Enrolled
in School, by Generation and Region**

Region	Generation			Regional Total
	First	Second	Third +	
Bay Area	42	27	42	38
Central Coast	78	8	30	45
Inland Empire	52	45	47	48
Los Angeles County	56	35	40	44
Orange County	59	24	38	42
Sacramento Metro	36	39	48	46
San Diego	57	30	40	41
San Joaquin Valley	58	48	48	51

SOURCES: Author's calculations from the 1997–2000 October
CPS.

Schools also keep track of the numbers of students who are recent immigrants to the United States (arrived within the last three years).[3] Approximately 4.5 percent of the state's students are recent immigrants

---

[3]These data are collected as a part of Title III of the Federal Elementary and Secondary Education Act (ESEA) under the Emergency Immigrant Education Program (EIEP). See the appendix for more detail.

(Figure 5.6). The greatest percentage of recent immigrants is found in Los Angeles County, followed by the Bay Area, Orange County, and San Diego. Statewide, over 60 percent of students who are recent immigrants come from Mexico and Central America, slightly more than 20 percent come from an Asian or Pacific Island nation, and about 15 percent come from elsewhere (Figure 5.7). The Bay Area, however, has approximately equal numbers of Mexican/Central American and Asian recent immigrant students. The Central Coast region has the highest percentage of Mexican/Central American immigrants—nearly 90 percent. A very high proportion of recent immigrant students in the Sacramento Metro region originate from some regions other than Asia or Mexico/Central America (44 percent), and it is the most common group for the region.

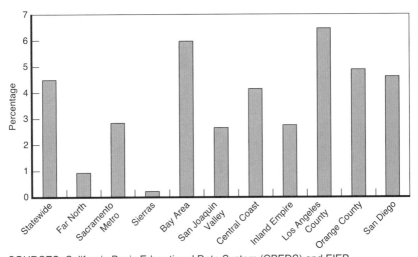

SOURCES: California Basic Educational Data System (CBEDS) and EIEP.
NOTE: See the appendix for more details.

Figure 5.6—Percentage of California Students in Grades 6–12 Who Are Recent Immigrants, by Region, 2000–2001

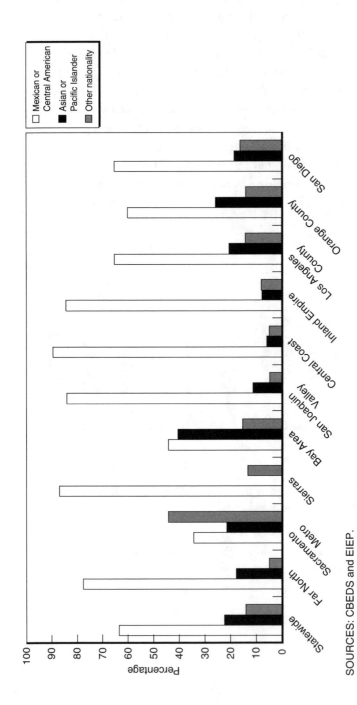

SOURCES: CBEDS and EIEP.
NOTE: See the appendix for more details.

Figure 5.7—National Origins of California Recent Immigrant Students in Grades 6–12, by Region, 2000–2001

Students who are a part of the Migration Education Program provide another measure of the well-being of immigrant youth.[4] It is important to know where the students are because they are likely to need special services at their schools. Also, they are likely to change schools (and school districts) often and may be more likely than other children of immigrants to have limited English language abilities.

The highest proportion of migrant students is found in the Central Coast region (16% in grades 6–8 and 15% in grades 9–12) (Figure 5.8). A high proportion of San Joaquin Valley students are also migrant students (12% in grades 6 through 8 and 10% in grades 9–12). Elsewhere in the state, percentages are much lower—less than 2 percent of students everywhere but the Far North and San Diego regions. In general, there are lower percentages of migrant students in grades 9–12 than in grades 6–8. There are two possible reasons. The first is that migrant youth who come to the United States to work may not be as easy for the program to find. The second possibility is that children of migrant workers are younger and therefore more likely to be found in middle school than in high school.

Regionally, some interesting patterns emerge in educational attainment for 19 to 24 year olds. The Bay Area has by far the highest percentage of youth with college degrees—one in seven has at least a B.A., although San Diego may not be statistically different in this regard (Figure 5.9). Only 1 percent of Bay Area youth have less than a ninth grade education. The Central Coast, however, has some of the most and least educated youth. Nearly 10 percent have less than a ninth grade education, but 68 percent have at least some college. Only the Bay Area (63%) and San Diego (63%) come close to matching the Central Coast on the high end, and neither have many very poorly educated youth. The San Joaquin Valley (9%) and Los Angeles County (8%) are the

---

[4]This program serves students under age 22 without a high school degree who are members of a family that performs migrant agricultural or fishing labor and have moved looking for work in the last three years. (See the appendix for more detail.) The students who are counted as migrant students may not be foreign-born, or even children of the foreign-born; however, most migrant laborers in California are foreign-born. Even youth who moved to the United States looking for work who have never attended school here are eligible for services.

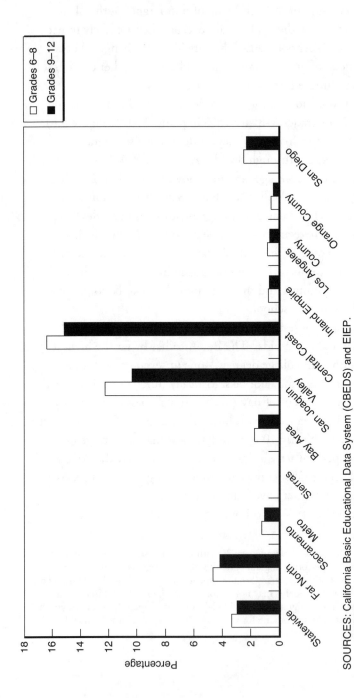

SOURCES: California Basic Educational Data System (CBEDS) and EIEP.

NOTE: See the appendix for more details.

Figure 5.8—Percentage of California Students in Migrant Education Program, by Grade and Region, 2000–2001

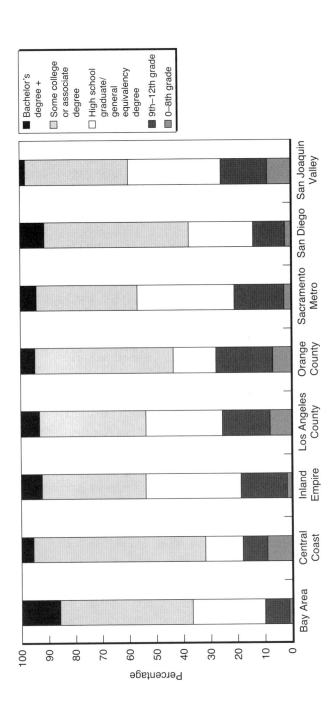

SOURCES: Author's calculations from the 1997–2001 March CPS.

Figure 5.9—Educational Attainment of California Youth Ages 19 to 24, by Region

75

regions that closely match the Central Coast on the low end. A number of regions have a large proportion of youth who did not complete high school. The Inland Empire, Los Angeles and Orange Counties, and the San Joaquin Valley each have over 25 percent of youth ages 19 to 24 without high school degrees.

Despite many poor outcomes for San Joaquin Valley youth, that region does not stand out in its measure of youth inactivity— approximately 6 percent of youth are inactive (not working, in school, or parenting), which is the same as the state average of 6 percent (Figure 5.10). However, in the Sacramento Metro region, over 10 percent of youth are inactive. Inactivity rates are higher in Los Angeles County, the Sacramento Metro region, and the San Joaquin Valley than in the other regions, most of which have inactivity rates of 3 in 100.

Regionally, there are vast differences in the fertility rates among youth. The first column of Table 5.4 displays the teen birth rate for each region, and subsequent columns display rates for each racial and ethnic group. Nearly 70 in 1,000 teens give birth each year in the San Joaquin Valley, which is well above the state average of 47. Hispanic teen fertility is exceedingly high in the region: 96. Rates of Hispanic teen childbearing in the Central Coast are only slightly higher than at the state level.

Blacks have the highest rates of external mortality nearly everywhere, with the exception of Orange County (Table 5.5). Relative to other racial and ethnic groups, blacks in the Bay Area and in Los Angeles County fare extremely poorly. For example, in the Bay Area, blacks have rates of externally caused mortality in excess of three times those of the next highest groups. Hispanics experience their highest rates of mortality in the Inland Empire and San Joaquin Valley. Asians also have their highest rates of mortality in the San Joaquin Valley. Indeed, the San Joaquin Valley is notable in that all racial and ethnic groups have fairly high and nearly equal levels of externally caused mortality.

Immigrant youth are a sizable presence in the San Joaquin Valley and the Central Coast, in addition to their large presence in Los Angeles and Orange Counties. The racial and ethnic composition of immigrant youth varies by region, as does their well-being.

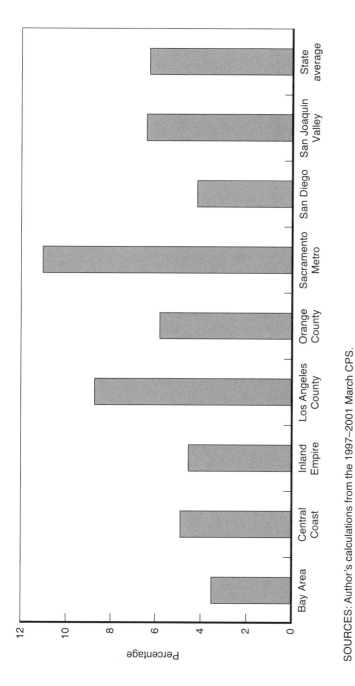

SOURCES: Author's calculations from the 1997–2001 March CPS.

Figure 5.10—Percentage of California Youth Ages 16 to 24 Who Are Inactive, by Region

Table 5.4

Teen Birth Rates for California Young Women Ages 15 to 19, by Region and Race/Ethnicity, 2000

Region	Total	Hispanic	White	Asian	Black
Far North	40	67	34	50	52
Sacramento Metro	37	69	26	33	74
San Joaquin Valley	69	96	42	53	91
Sierras	33	64	28	(a)	(a)
Bay Area	33	75	14	14	61
Central Coast	42	80	15	20	44
Los Angeles County	50	75	15	9.5	58
Orange County	39	81	14	9	40
Inland Empire	56	80	36	17	71
San Diego	45	82	20	19	65
State total	47	75	22	14	61

SOURCE: Johnson (2003).

NOTE: Rates are per 1,000.

aRates are not calculated for base populations of less than 200.

Table 5.5

External Mortality Rates for California Youth Ages 13 to 24, by Region and Race/Ethnicity, 2000–2001

Region	Hispanic	Asian	Black	White
Bay Area	31	24	96	30
Central Coast	48	20	(a)	29
Far North	48	(a)	(a)	56
Inland Empire	56	30	(a)	51
Los Angeles	48	24	116	35
Orange	26	22	26	32
Sacramento	44	34	59	37
San Diego	34	30	61	41
San Joaquin	51	57	64	53
State total	44	28	87	40

SOURCE: Author's calculations from 2000–2001 California Vital Statistics and Census 2000 SF1.

NOTE: Rates are per 1,000.

aRates are not calculated for base populations of less than 20,000.

School enrollment varies tremendously by region. Nearly 80 percent of immigrant youth living in the Central Coast are not enrolled in school. Many immigrant youth in that region are likely there for agricultural work and are unlikely to enroll in school. For San Joaquin Valley youth, generation does not appear to be related to enrollment— only about half of youth of any generation are enrolled in school at ages 16 to 24. Among recent immigrants who do enroll in school, over 60 percent are Mexican or Central American. As we might expect, the majority of nonnative English speakers in the public school system are native Spanish speakers. Regionally, nonnative English speakers are found in large proportions in Los Angeles (over 50%) and Orange Counties (40%). The share of English Learner students is high in both Los Angeles and Orange Counties as well as in the Central Coast region.

Youth in the San Joaquin Valley are most likely to be in families receiving welfare, whereas youth in the Central Coast are the least likely. However, the gap between the percentage of poor youth and the percentage of youth who receive welfare is largest in the Central Coast. This report finds health insurance coverage to be quite low among youth in Los Angeles.

Regional variations in resources for youth and their families indicate that the areas with large concentrations of recent immigrants generally have youth populations with low levels of resources. In particular, Los Angeles County, the San Joaquin Valley, the San Diego region, and the Central Coast have a high proportion of youth who are poor, lack health insurance, and have low levels of educational attainment.

6. Conclusions and Policy Directions

Immigrant youth do not typically receive much research attention. Younger youth are studied as a part of families or as a subset of children, and older youth are grouped with adults. However, moving from childhood to adulthood is a process that spans many years and should be studied in its own right, especially among immigrants. During this transition, young people can make many choices that have large positive or negative consequences for later life, but eventual outcomes will also depend on family background characteristics that youth cannot choose. In examining California's cross section of immigrant youth, this report takes a snapshot of a number of socioeconomic outcomes for all of the state's young people of each racial and ethnic group and compares outcomes across them.

A promising finding of the report is just how similar immigrant youth who arrive in the United States by the age of 10 are to native-born youth of their own race and ethnicity. By ages 19 to 24, these youth have educational attainment levels, school enrollment figures, language skills, and rates of family formation similar to those of the native-born. Similarly, Asian immigrant youth who arrive after age 10 fare well because it appears that many of them come to the United States to attend school. Immigrant youth who are educated in the United States benefit from the same set of policy recommendations that will help second- and third-generation youth. Policymakers can find these students enrolled in California's schools, where we can address school completion, family planning, and the transition to work.

Outcomes for Hispanic immigrant youth who arrive after age 10 are alarming. These youth will have to struggle to build economic security for themselves and their families. They are poor, lack health insurance, rarely speak English fluently, have low levels of educational attainment and school enrollment, and are likely to have already started families.

Addressing this last group's problems will not be easy. They are not in school and may never have attended school in the United States. Estimates from the 2000 Census for California indicate that nearly 8,000 Hispanic immigrants ages 13 to 15 and 65,000 Hispanic immigrants ages 16 to 18 are not enrolled in school. Furthermore, many are likely to lack legal status and will not be eligible for TANF. As they begin to have children born in the United States, however, their families will become eligible. Increasing English language skills and access to education are probably the most critical policy priorities.

There are at least three different ways to target services to these youth. The first is through their place of work: Approximately 80 percent of Hispanic men and nearly 50 percent of Hispanic women ages 19 to 24 who arrived in the United States after age 10 are working. Public-private partnerships of county-level Workforce Investment Boards (WIBs) with employers of large numbers of immigrants have had some success (Hill and Gera, 2000). However, only employers who need their immigrant employees to interact with English-speaking customers may have any incentive to engage in these partnerships. For example, hotels offer spoken English instruction to their maid staff. Unfortunately, as this report suggests, these immigrant youth face the largest obstacles to becoming economically secure in agricultural areas. In such places as the Central Coast and the San Joaquin Valley, public entities might face higher hurdles to forming partnerships with employers.

Second, adult education and language training could be targeted to these youth through their children's schools. California already has a program called Healthy Start, which operates through some of its elementary schools. This program aims to reach poor families through their children.

Third, the MEP, part of the Federal Title I Program, also assists out-of-school youth up to age 21. MEP tries to assist both those who drop out of school and those who have never entered school. The program contacts out-of-school youth through their younger siblings (who are enrolled in schools), through neighborhood community centers, and from other places where immigrant youth may congregate, such as labor pick-up locations. Programs include earning a GED in Spanish and assistance in placement in English language education programs.

This report also finds that third-generation Hispanics still fare poorly relative to third-generation white youth. Third-generation Hispanics likely lag whites and Asians in educational attainment, and current school enrollment does not suggest that these gaps will close anytime soon. Despite high levels of employment, Hispanic third-generation youth are the least likely to have health insurance coverage. They are also the most likely of all youth to have started their own families.

The analysis of this report identifies two important areas for future PPIC research. First, policy research on youth who arrive in their teenage years is important because those youth represent a substantial share of California's youth, their children will be a substantial share of the next generation of Californians, and they are faring poorly, particularly Hispanics. Second, the data used in this report do not allow us to measure intergenerational progress. Clearly, such progress is of utmost importance because nearly half of all Californians today are first- or second-generation immigrants. The well-being of the population, health of political institutions, and strength of the economy depend on the successful integration of these new Americans. Future PPIC research will investigate intergenerational progress and identify key policy areas for promoting progress.

Appendix

Data Sources

This appendix details the data sources used in this report. The majority of the tables and figures presented rely on the Current Population Survey. We describe the CPS and our use of it here. We then discuss the school data and mortality data also used in this report.

The Current Population Survey

The CPS is a national survey of approximately 50,000 households (5,000 in California) collected monthly. The CPS includes a host of demographic and economic variables, such as the country of birth and year of arrival for each household member. Parents' birthplaces are also collected, making it possible to distinguish among second- and third- (plus)-generation youth. Our sample of 11,000 Californian youth (from the 1997–2001 March CPS) is large enough to disaggregate California's youth by race/ethnicity, immigrant generation, age, and region. As is evident from Table A.1, the sample of American Indian youth is too small for separate analysis, and the sample of California's black youth population is too small to disaggregate by generation. For the most part, CPS data analyzed in this report come from the March Annual Demographic Survey (1997–2001), although some analyses use data from the October School Enrollment Supplement (1997–2000), the October Computer Ownership/Internet Supplement (1997), and the November Voting and Registration Surveys (1998 and 2000). All results reflect the use of the CPS person-level weights.

Following Johnson (2002), we divide California into ten regions, nine of which are adequately enough covered by the CPS to report here (Tables A.2 and A.3). The 30 counties covered by the CPS in the years 1997–2001 provide representation for approximately 95 percent of the state's population as measured in the 2000 Census.

Table A.1

CPS Sample Sizes of California Youth

Generation	13–15	16–18	19–24	Grand Total
Hispanic				
First, arrived age 18+			341	341
First, arrived ages 10–17	39	157	681	877
First, arrived age <10	349	311	478	1,138
Second, 2 foreign-born parents	675	590	750	2,015
Second, 1 foreign-born parent	186	137	197	520
Third +	323	319	536	1,178
Total	1,572	1,514	2,983	6,069
Non-Hispanic American Indian				
First, arrived age 18+				0
First, arrived ages 10–17			3	3
First, arrived age <10			5	5
Second, 2 foreign-born parents	4	2	2	8
Second, 1 foreign-born parent	1	1	1	3
Third +	16	16	23	55
Total	21	19	34	74
Non-Hispanic Asian-Pacific Islander				
First, arrived age 18+			48	48
First, arrived ages 10–17	17	40	107	164
First, arrived age <10	68	89	168	325
Second, 2 foreign-born parents	136	137	139	412
Second, 1 foreign-born parent	31	32	24	87
Third +	34	31	39	104
Total	286	329	525	1,140
Non-Hispanic Black				
First, arrived age 18+			5	5
First, arrived ages 10–17	3	5	8	16
First, arrived age <10	7	1	13	21
Second, 2 foreign-born parents	1	2	4	7
Second, 1 foreign-born parent	8	3	7	18
Third +	155	132	200	487
Total	174	143	237	554
Non-Hispanic White				
First, arrived age 18+			28	28
First, arrived ages 10–17	11	18	45	74
First, arrived age <10	29	29	76	134
Second, 2 foreign-born parents	47	54	72	173
Second, 1 foreign-born parent	96	86	101	283
Third +	833	706	1,365	2,904
Total	1,016	893	1,687	3,596
Grand total	3,069	2,898	5,466	11,433

SOURCE: Author's calculations from the 1997–2001 March CPS

Table A.2

Regional Definitions

CPS Counties		Counties Without CPS Representation	
Far North			
Butte	Sutter	Colusa	Neveda
		Del Norte	Plumas
		Glenn	Shasta
		Humboldt	Sierra
		Lake	Siskiyou
		Lassen	Tehama
		Medocino	Trinity
		Modoc	Yuba
Sacramento Metro			
El Dorado	Sacramento		
Placer	Yolo		
Sierras			
		Alpine	Mariposa
		Amador	Mono
		Calveras	Tuolumne
		Inyo	
Bay Area			
Alameda	San Mateo		
Contra Costa	Santa Clara		
Marin	Solano		
Napa	Sonoma		
San Francisco			
San Joaquin Valley			
Fresno	San Joaquin	Kings	Madera
Kern	Stanislaus		
Merced	Tulare		
Central Coast			
Monterey	Santa Barbara	San Benito	Santa Cruz
San Luis Obispo			
Inland Empire			
Riverside	San Bernardino		
Los Angeles County			
Los Angeles			
Orange County			
Orange			
San Diego			
San Diego		Imperial	

NOTE: Ventura County is available in the CPS but is not included in this analysis.

Table A.3

Regional Sample Sizes (Excluding Ventura County)

	Generation			
Region	First	Second	Third +	Total
Bay Area	385	393	733	1,511
Central Coast	155	86	269	510
Far North	32	37	144	213
Inland Empire	125	199	502	826
Los Angeles County	1,685	1,877	1,398	4,960
Orange County	227	177	255	659
Sacramento Metro	47	66	282	395
San Diego	165	238	404	807
San Joaquin Valley	324	387	572	1,283
Unknown	12	6	65	83
Grand total	3,157	3,466	4,624	11,247

SOURCE: Author's calculations from the 1997–2001 March CPS.

School Data

Language Census

The Language Census (LC) is a school-level summary maintained by the Educational Demographics Unit in the California Department of Education (CDE). Each March, the census enumerates the number of English learner and fluent English-proficient students in California public schools (K–12) by grade and primary language other than English.[1] This analysis calculates overall numbers of non–English-speaking students from the EL and FEP counts for each school, as well as percentages of total students for each category. Because these data are collected in March and the enrollment data are collected in October, the percentages of students who are EL and FEP are estimates rather than exact measures.

---

[1] EL students are nonnative-English speakers who have been determined to lack the clearly defined English language skills of listening comprehension, speaking, reading, and writing necessary to succeed in the school's regular instructional programs, based on the state-approved oral language assessment procedures (grades K–12) and literacy assessment in grades 3–12. FEP students are nonnative-English speakers who have met the district criteria for determining proficiency in English, either at the initial identification or upon redesignation from EL to FEP.

Emergency Immigrant Education Program (EIEP)

This census of immigrant students who arrived in the United States within the past three years is conducted as part of the requirements for local educational agencies (LEAs) to receive federal funding for eligible immigrant students under the No Child Left Behind Act of 2002, Title III (formerly Improving America's School Act, Title VII, Part C). Both public school and private school students (through a public LEA) are eligible for funding if the LEA meets the following conditions: (1) It enrolls at least 500 eligible immigrant pupils and/or (2) the enrollment of eligible immigrant pupils represents at least 3 percent of the LEA's total enrollment.[2] If a LEA has eligible immigrant students but does not have enough students to qualify under the threshold described above, it will not participate in the census, which may result in an undercount of recent immigrant students.

Migrant Education Program (MEP)

MEP students are counted under Part C of Title I of the Elementary and Secondary Education Act and by state laws that define the administrative framework for delivering MEP services in California. A migrant student is defined by federal law as "a migrant agricultural worker or a migrant fisher (as defined in Section 1309 of the statute) OR has a parent, spouse, or guardian who is a migrant agricultural worker or a migrant fisher; AND performs, or has a parent, spouse, or guardian who performs, qualifying agricultural or fishing employment as a principal means of livelihood (34 CFR 200.40(c), (e), and (f)); AND has moved within the preceding 36 months to obtain, or to accompany or join a parent, spouse, or guardian to obtain, temporary or seasonal employment in agricultural or fishing work; AND has moved from one school district to another."[3] The data contain both attending students and nonattending students. We use only the attending students in our calculations. Students who attended more than one school or were enrolled in more than one grade during the given school year were

---

[2]In practice, very few immigrant students are in private schools.

[3]http://www.ed.gov/offices/OESE/MEP/PrelimGuide/pt2b.html (downloaded 5/17/02).

89

counted once for each school or grade. Thus, there is some duplicate counting of migrant students, which may result in percentages of total enrollment exceeding 100. We top-code any migrant percentages that exceed 100 to 100 percent. Migrant students might be immigrants or recent immigrants or they might not be immigrants at all. We have no way of knowing exactly what percentage of migrant students are native-born U.S. citizens from the data collected by CDE.

Mortality Data

Counts of deaths for the years 2000 and 2001 are from the California Vital Statistics Death Records. Death records contain mortality data for every death that occurred in California as well as deaths to California residents that occurred outside the state. Death records include cause of death, the decedent's place of birth, current place of residence, race and ethnicity, sex, and age. Age-specific death rates are created by dividing the counts of deaths to youth of a particular age, race or ethnicity, and nativity by population counts of youth in that category. Population counts are from the 2000 Census (SF3). When a population is smaller than 20,000 individuals, we do not report mortality rates. We use proportions for the foreign-born youth from the 1997–2001 CPS to estimate the population of the foreign- and native-born by race and ethnicity. The death records and Census data both allow for the choice of mixed race; the CPS does not. Therefore, estimates of mortality that include place of birth and race/ethnicity include a small margin of error because we do not know what share of the foreign-born population of youth might have been in the multiracial category if that choice had been offered in the CPS. Overall, somewhat less than 6 percent of California youth identify as mixed-race, and the proportion is somewhat higher among the native-born.

Bibliography

Aguayo, Jennifer E., Richard Brown, Michael A. Rodriguez, and Lia Margolis, "Important Health Care Issues for California Latinos: Health Insurance and Health Status," UCLA Center for Health Policy Research, Los Angeles, California, January 2003.

Bean, Frank D., C. G. Swicegood, and R. Berg, "Mexican-Origin Fertility: New Patterns and Interpretations," *Social Science Quarterly*, Vol. 81, 2000.

Brandon, Peter David, "The Living Arrangements of Children in Immigrant Families in the United States," *International Migration Review*, Vol. 36, No. 2, Summer 2002.

Brown, Richard E., et al., "The State of Health Insurance in California: Findings from the 2001 California Health Interview Survey," UCLA Center for Health Policy Research, Los Angeles, California, June 2002.

Carnevale, Anthony P., Richard A. Fry, and B. Lindsay Lowell, "Understanding, Speaking, Reading, Writing, and Earnings in the Immigrant Labor Market," *AEA Papers and Proceedings*, Vol. 91, No. 2, 2001.

Citrin, Jack, and Benjamin Highton, *How Race, Ethnicity, and Immigration Shape the California Electorate,* Public Policy Institute of California, San Francisco, California, 2002.

Citro, Constance F., and Robert T. Michaels, eds., "Introduction and Overview," in *Measuring Poverty: A New Approach*, National Academy Press, Washington, D.C., 1995.

Driscoll, Anne K., "Risk of High School Dropout Among Immigrant and Native Hispanic Youth," *International Migration Review*, Vol. 33, No. 4, Winter 1999.

Eschbach, Karl, and Christina Gomez, "Choosing Hispanic Identity: Ethnic Identity Switching among Respondents to High School and Beyond," *Social Science Quarterly*, Vol. 79, No. 1, March 1998.

Fix, Michael, and Wendy Zimmermann, "All Under One Roof: Mixed-Status Families in an Era of Reform," *International Migration Review*, Vol. 35, No. 2, 2001.

Fry, Richard, "Latinos in Higher Education: Many Enroll, Too Few Graduate," Pew Hispanic Center, Washington, D.C., 2002.

Furstenberg, Frank F., Maureen R. Waller, and Hongyu Wang, *The Well-Being of California's Children*, Public Policy Institute of California, San Francisco, California, 2003.

Garfinkel, Irvin, and Sarah McLanahan, *Single Mothers and Their Children: A New American Dilemma*, The Urban Institute Press, Washington, D.C., 1986.

Gonzalez, Arturo, "The Education and Wages of Immigrant Children: The Impact of Age at Arrival," *Economics of Education Review*, Vol. 22, No. 2, 2003.

Gonzalez, Arturo, "The Acquisition and Labor Market Value of Four English Skills: New Evidence from NALS," *Contemporary Economic Policy*, Vol. 18, No. 3, 2000.

Grogger, Jeffrey, and Stephen J. Trejo, *Falling Behind or Moving Up? The Intergenerational Progress of Mexican Americans*, Public Policy Institute of California, San Francisco, California, 2002.

Hayes-Bautista, David E., "The Latino Health Research Agenda," in Marcelo M. Suarez-Orozco and Mariela M. Paez, eds., *Latinos: Remaking America*, University of California Press, Berkeley, California, 2002.

Hill, Laura E., "Connections Between U.S. Female Migration and Family Formation and Dissolution," *Migraciones Internacionales*, Vol. 2, No. 3, 2004 (forthcoming).

Hill, Laura, and Jennifer Gera, "San Mateo County Job Creation Investment Fund: Summary Report," The Sphere Institute, Burlingame, California, 2000.

Hill, Laura E., and Hans P. Johnson, *Understanding the Future of Californians' Fertility: The Role of Immigrants*, The Public Policy Institute of California, San Francisco, California, 2002.

Hill, Laura E., and Joseph M. Hayes, "California's Newest Immigrants," *California Counts,* Vol. 5, No. 2, Public Policy Institute of California, San Francisco, California, 2003.

Jamieson, Amie, Andrea Curry, and Gladys Martinez, "School Enrollment in the United States—Social and Economic Characteristics of Students, October 1999," U.S. Census Bureau, P20-533, 2001.

Johnson, Hans P., "A State of Diversity: Demographic Trends in California's Regions," *California Counts*, Vol. 3, No. 5, Public Policy Institute of California, San Francisco, California, 2002.

Johnson, Hans P., "Maternity Before Maturity: Teen Birth Rates in California," *California Counts*, Vol. 4, No. 3, Public Policy Institute of California, San Francisco, California, 2003.

Kids Count Data Book, The Annie E. Casey Foundation, 2002.

McLanahan, Sara S., "Parent Absence or Poverty: Which Matters More?" in G. Duncan and J. Brooks-Gunn, eds., *Consequences of Growing Up Poor,* Russell Sage Press, New York," 1997, pp. 35–48.

New York Forum for Child Health, the New York Academy of Medicine, and the University of California, San Francisco, "Challenges Associated with Applying for Health Insurance Among Latina Mothers in California, Florida, and New York," New York, New York, December 2002.

Peete, Cynthia, "The Importance of Place of Residence in Health Outcomes Research: How Does Living in an Ethnic Enclave Affect Low Birthweight Deliveries for Hispanic Mothers?" unpublished dissertation, University of California, Berkeley, 1999.

Portes, Alejandro, and Dag MacLeod, "What Shall I Call Myself? Hispanic Identity Formation in the Second Generation," *Ethnic and Racial Studies*, Vol. 19, No. 3, 1996.

Portes, Alejandro, and Rubén G. Rumbaut, *Immigrant America: A Portrait,* 2nd ed., University of California Press, Berkeley, 1996.

Portes, Alejandro, and Rubén G. Rumbaut, *Legacies: The Story of the Immigrant Second Generation,* University of California Press, Berkeley, 2001.

Powers, Daniel A., "Transitions into Idleness Among White, Black, and Hispanic Youth: Some Determinants and Policy Implications of Weak Labor Force Attachment," *Sociological Perspectives*, Vol. 37, No. 2, 1994, pp. 183–201.

Powers, Mary G., William Seltzer, and Jing Shi, "Gender Differences in the Occupational Status of Undocumented Immigrants in the United States: Experiences Before and After Legalization," *International Migration Review*, Vol. 32, No. 4, 1998.

Ramakrishnan, S. Karthick, "Second Generation Immigrants? The '2.5 Generation' in the United States," *Social Science Quarterly*, Vol. 85, No. 2, 2004.

Reardon-Anderson, Jane, Randolph Capps, and Michael E. Fix, "The Health and Well-Being of Children in Immigrant Families," The Urban Institute, New Federalism: National Survey of America's Families, No. B-52, Washington, D.C., November 2002.

Reed, Deborah, and Richard Van Swearingen, "Poverty in California: Levels, Trends, and Demographic Dimensions," *California Counts*, Vol. 3, No. 3, Public Policy Institute of California, San Francisco, California, 2001.

Reyes, Belinda I., ed. *A Portrait of Race and Ethnicity in California: An Assessment of Social and Economic Well-Being*, Public Policy Institute of California, San Francisco, California, 2001.

Shetterly, Susan M., Judith Baxter, Lynn D. Mason, and Richard F. Hamman, "Self-Rated Health among Hispanic vs. Non-Hispanic White Adults: The San Luis Valley Health and Aging Study," *American Journal of Public Health*, Vol. 86, No. 12, 1996.

Smith, James P., "Assimilation Across the Latino Generations," *AEA Papers and Proceedings*, Vol. 93, No. 2, May 2003.

Sorenson, Susan B., and Haikang Shen, "Youth Suicide Trends in California: An Examination of Immigrant and Ethnic Group Risk," *Suicide and Life-Threatening Behavior*, Vol. 26, No. 2, Summer 1996.

State of California, Department of Finance, *Race/Ethnic Population with Age and Sex Detail, 1970–2040*, Sacramento, California, December 1998.

Tafoya, Sonya, "The Linguistic Landscape of California's Schools," *California Counts*, Vol. 3, No. 4, Public Policy Institute of California, San Francisco, California, 2002.

Vandivere, Sharon, Kristin Moore, and Brett Brown, "Child Well-Being at the Outset of Welfare Reform: An Overview of the Nation and 13 States," The Urban Institute, Assessing the New Federalism Policy Brief B-23, Washington, D.C., 2000.

Vernez, Georges, and Lee Mizell, "Goal: To Double the Rate of Hispanics Earning a B.A.," prepared for Hispanic Scholarship Fund. RAND Education, Center for Research on Immigration Policy, Santa Monica, Calfornia, 2001.

Wilson, William Julius, *When Work Disappears: The World of the New Urban Poor,* Alfred A. Knopf, New York, 1997.

About the Author

LAURA E. HILL

Laura E. Hill is a research fellow at the Public Policy Institute of California, where she conducts research on immigrants, international migration, race and ethnicity, and youth. Before joining PPIC as a research fellow, she was a research associate at The SPHERE Institute and a National Institute of Aging postdoctoral fellow. She has a Ph.D. in demography from the University of California, Berkeley.

Related PPIC Publications

The Well-Being of California's Children
Frank F. Furstenberg, Maureen R. Waller, and Hongyu Wang

"California's Newest Immigrants"
California Counts: Population Trends and Profiles
Volume 5, Number 2, November 2003
Laura E. Hill and Joseph M. Hayes

Understanding the Future of Californians' Fertility: The Role of Immigrants
Laura E. Hill and Hans P. Johnson

"The Linguistic Landscape of California Schools"
California Counts: Population Trends and Profiles
Volume 3, Number 4, February 2002
Sonya M. Tafoya

A Portrait of Race and Ethnicity in California: An Assessment of Social and Economic Well-Being
Belinda I. Reyes (editor), Jennifer Cheng, Elliot Currie, Daniel Frakes, Hans P. Johnson, Elizabeth Bronwen Macro, Deborah Reed, Belinda I. Reyes, José Signoret, Joanne Spetz (contributors)

PPIC publications may be ordered by phone or from our website
(800) 232-5343 [mainland U.S.]
(415) 291-4400 [Canada, Hawaii, overseas]
www.ppic.org